The Mystery of Preaching

James Black

edited by

Peter Cotterell

ZONDERVAN PUBLISHING HOUSE
OF THE ZONDERVAN CORPORATION
GRAND RAPIDS, MICHIGAN 49506

THE MYSTERY OF PREACHING

Revised edition, 1977, published by
Marshall, Morgan & Scott
London, England
ISBN 0-551-05563-4

Published in 1978 by The Zondervan Corporation
Grand Rapids, Michigan
ISBN 0-310-36991-6

Printed in the United States of America

Preface

I have called this book 'The Mystery of Preaching' because, in spite of all the advice I have tried to crush within these covers, great preaching will always remain a mystery, not least to the preacher himself. It is bound up ultimately in the greater mystery of personality.

I forestall even the kindly critic by assuring him that this is a volume of lectures, not essays. I publish them *as lectures*—and I publish them only because the Trust under which they were delivered demands that I should! Otherwise, had I my own will, they should have been decently buried after their birth.

I have refrained from disguising or amending their lecture form. I believe that whatever may be typically good in a lecture is only likely to be ruined by literary tinkering. Rather than fall between two stools, I have chosen to sit down solidly on one! And so I have studiously maintained, almost unaltered, the free style of address, which alone gives a lecture any point or appeal.

My choice of form accounts also for the retention of some illustrations and personal experiences, which one might use freely in speech but might not sit down in cold blood to put on paper. My hope is that any liveliness likely to have pervaded the spoken lectures may not have escaped entirely from the printed page.

The book in the first instance represents the *Warrack Lectures*, delivered to the students of the United Free Church Colleges at Edinburgh, Glasgow, and Aberdeen in the spring of 1923. Lectures one to six were thus used in such parts as was possible within the prescribed hour.

The whole eight lectures were again delivered under *The James Sprunt Foundation* at Union Theological Seminary, Richmond, U.S.A., in the autumn of the same year. Of this visit and the unexampled kindness of many friends, I have choice memories: and I should like, thus publicly, to thank these gracious people of the

South for many undeserved courtesies to one within their gates, typical, however, of their traditional chivalry.

I had also the pleasure and honour of delivering the first lecture as the Inaugural Speech at Princeton Theological Seminary, and afterwards as a special lecture at Union Theological Seminary, New York.

Need I say that while I have drawn largely from my own experience in these lectures—perhaps annoyingly to many readers—I have purloined right and left any hint or suggestion that came to my hand. These appropriations are too numerous for me to make any adequate acknowledgement. But in every instance I have tried to speak out of my own heart and experience. If thereby I lead any of my readers to question what I say, I shall have served a useful purpose.

Finally, I should like to disclaim any right to advise, as if I were one who had always practised what I preach. I have tried to give, not my own habit, but my own *ideal*, a distinction with a real difference! Indeed, so far as my own work goes, I feel so diffident about my ability to speak that had I been asked to furnish a subtitle to these lectures, I should have been tempted to express it thus humorously, 'How to do it, by one who doesn't know.'

I have to thank my varied audiences here and in America for great and unmerited kindness, and my friends, the Rev. Gavin J. Tait, M.A., of Paisley, and Mr. Charles F. Ridland, S.S.C., of Edinburgh, for corrections and suggestions in revising the proofs.

J. B.

St. George's United Free Church
Edinburgh
1924

NOTE ON REVISED EDITION

In this revised edition changes have been restricted to such matters as punctuation and layout although the careful reader will discover a few minor textual emendations (e.g. Sunday school for Sabbath school).

F. P. C.

The London Bible College

Contents

1 To-day is Not Yesterday

Change indeed is painful: yet ever needful: and if Memory have its force and worth, so also has Hope.
CARLYLE, *Characterists*

INTRODUCTION

I understand that the intention of the founder of this lectureship is that a man from the active ministry, not too inexperienced and not too antiquated, should be invited here to discuss with you the common problems of our work. I accepted this charge with diffidence, for I remembered that my audience would be composed mainly of professors and students. Somehow, I early lost my fear of the professors. Experience such as theirs makes men wonderfully kind and tolerant. And further, if the truth be told, I recalled the hoary gibe that within a year or two every self-respecting professor forgets all he ever knew about preaching!

But I am still possessed by my fear of the student. Remembering our own thoughts in college days, I quail before your omniscience and your beautiful assurance. I remember, penitently enough, how easy preaching seemed to us in those days, how sweeping was our criticism of what we called 'futilities', how generous and wholesale were our easy schemes for the world's reformation, and especially with what tolerant scorn we regarded a lectureship on this special subject. Perhaps I am about to be hoist with my own petard, a type of poetic justice. But if it makes any appeal to you, not for me but for my subject, I should like to say quite frankly that I am a humbler and sadder man than I was twenty years ago.

My hope is to treat our subject as practically and helpfully as possible, in line with the founder's wishes. You are here not so much to acquire learning, as to use that learning, when acquired, for preaching purposes. If any workman in the world has a direct aim, you have: and let no false views of learning obscure this in your own mind. You cannot put too high a value on study and the pursuit of knowledge, unless you regard them as ends in themselves. For us as ministers, ambassadors for God, everything must subserve the higher end of usefulness, in making us more accurate thinkers, trained men, preachers and teachers of influence and power. A theological college must never be allowed to ruin a good preacher, or water down his enthusiasm. Unless your aim here is intensely practical in the best sense, this institution defeats its own purpose. A college, first and last, is a factory for preachers.

With this practical aim in my mind, I took two precautions. In the first instance, I thought it insufficient merely to recall the difficulties and problems which faced me at the beginning of my own ministry: for as you will understand, a man is only too apt to forget what puzzled him twenty years ago. So I busied myself with some enquiries among young ministers and students, asking them plainly what type of question my lectures should attempt to answer, almost as if we were sitting together round the common-room fire. Here, for instance, are some of the topics suggested to me which I shall hope to consider in our later discussion. 'What should I aim at in writing and preaching sermons?' 'Tell us how we can best use the material and the gifts we have.' 'Sketch how we should handle the Bible for congregational preaching.' 'Should I try, straightway, to preach without a manuscript?' 'How can I best gain confidence in myself and my message?' This last question, by the way, only from the very humble man: some people never feel the difficulty. These are the types of question I shall try to answer in our discussions, for I shall be of little service here if I do not face the problems which press on you in your opening years.

I took a second precaution. I asked some layfolk, men and women, to give me their views of effective preaching. I believe that the pew, our chief sufferer, should have something to say on a matter like this. I asked these friends to tell me what type and style of address they liked best as hearers, the qualities they valued most in a sermon or a preacher, their views on the great mystery of pulpit impression and effectiveness, and even their ideas on such questions as the length and place of the sermon.

I know, of course, that the value of such opinions depends entirely on the judgment and experience of those who express them. Some people's views about sermons are as useful as their views about astronomy. But on that score at least, I satisfied myself.

Generally, as a result of this, I was struck with their appreciation of the high level of modern pulpit work. Some said—here we all bow our heads—that there are fewer unique preachers in our generation, men of arresting personality, but that the general plane of congregational preaching is immeasurably higher than ever before. I believe this is true. Principal Fairbairn once informed me that what impressed him most deeply in his holiday haunts was the general excellence of the average sermon he heard in the smallest country parish. As he himself put it, 'You will hear as fine a sermon in a Perthshire village as you will get any day in Edinburgh or London.'

Incidentally also, if I may give some general results here, I was astonished but pleased to find an almost unanimous preference for what we call expository preaching, where a text, passage, incident, chapter or book is chosen and its central truths explained, expounded and applied. Even in America, where purely topical preaching has largely captured the market, I find that this preference exists strongly amongst most thoughtful people. This, by the way, is a great comfort to the average preacher, for it shows a fine taste and appetite among our best hearers.

Further, from these answers I gained this, that the preaching quality my friends valued most was not dramatic power, nor great brilliance of thought or language, nor logical argument, nor passion, nor eloquence, but what, from lack of a better word, they called *interest*. (I try to define what interest is in lecture 2.) They desired that the preacher should engage and hold the mind with some truth or aspect of truth that has interest and bearing on human life, and should treat it in a living and gripping fashion. This also is a great comfort. Many of the other gifts are as much beyond our reach as the stars, and to strive after them is like baying at the moon. But with diligence and patience, most of us, I believe, can cultivate real human interest. If we only study ourselves and our fellow-men, the passions and longings that are our common heritage, our desires and limitations and failings, the needs and sorrows of the world, our links with the best and the worst, we shall not be far from the mark.

Such as they are, these are the precautions I took, lest I should be speaking only of casual aspects of our work and things of interest to myself alone, or lest, worst of all, I should be beating the air.

1. OUR NOBLEST SERVICE

Our general subject then is preaching, its problems and difficulties, preaching as the great function of our ministry. My first remark is ordinary enough, but yet goes down to the root of things—that if our work is worth doing at all, it is worth doing well. Ours is a great and magnificent service, and deserves the consecration of any gift we possess. To do our work half-heartedly is sheer ruin, for that in the end is tragedy to the man and the people alike. I cannot understand the minister who thinks his preaching may be done anyhow, or who slackly fails to perfect each gift of mind and expression for this high end. Surely there is no talent in us too fine to be used boldly for God's work. As George Herbert remarks, 'It is an ill mason that refuseth any stone.'

May I ask you, therefore, to resolve early to make your preaching the big business of your life. Not of course, to the exclusion or weakening of any other aspect of your work. The fact is, your other work, faithfully done, is the only way to enrich your preaching. It will give your word direction and point and vigour: it will give it blood. Apart from those who are constitutionally ineffective, most of the failures of the ministry are due to some sort of mental or spiritual slackness. I know of no sphere of labour where honesty, hard work, and honour with oneself tell more. Indeed, the astounding thing in the Church is the condoning patience of the people. If only a man gives his best, he will experience from the hands of any average congregation a loyalty that shames him in his own heart, and a love from simple souls that should make him better than his own best. Give your ministry, therefore, in college and afterwards, every gift of mind and soul, of thought and speech, of method and manner, which you can bring to the altar. I do not know a single man who has been faithful to himself and his calling who has been without his sufficient reward.

2. THE PLACE OF PREACHING

Some of you, at this point, may question the value and place commonly assigned to preaching. It is fashionable nowadays to assert that the sermon is too obtrusive and conspicuous in our Protestant worship. Everything else is preliminary, and the sermon is central. Other churches, as strong and historic, place the general rites and sacraments of Christianity in a finer prominence, and relegate preaching to its due significance or insignificance. My only answer is, not that we lessen the sacraments (for I believe we give them a worthy place in line with New Testament ideas), but that our ideal for the Church, first and last, is to have an informed people, intelligent in their own faith and instructed in truth. When you consider that preaching is the only opportunity many people have of learning Christian truth, a mere matter of an hour or two per week, you will agree that this is little enough, in all conscience, to train any congregation in the ways and mind of God.

As for the common contrast between preaching and worship—'Give us more worship and less preaching,' you know the cry—as for that, it is merely a parrot-cry. If worship is confessing sin, praising God, and glorifying Jesus as Lord—and what is it if it is not that?—how better can this be done than in a reverent address where the thoughts of the people are uplifted, where conscience is stirred, and the sublime goodness of God is plainly exposed? It may be the fault of my training and heritage, but to me preaching is the finest and fullest worship. Carlyle says that the essence of worship is 'transcendent wonder'. If so, then preaching is transcendent worship. It lifts men to God's feet.

I wish then to speak to you about preaching. Necessarily, throughout these lectures, I have to treat our subject as an art and craft, something which, like every art, has laws and rules to be known and practised. But while I am speaking about rules, I should like to state early that all the rules and methods ever laid down will not make a man a preacher, any more than a knowledge of the laws of poetry or painting will make a man a poet or an artist. But a poet without any art or rule is just so much wasted material; and a preacher without knowledge of his craft may be criminally ineffective.

In our profession, therefore, it is needful to know the laws of our art: if they do nothing more, they will at least save us from crude and expensive mistakes. Roger Ascham remarks in *The Scholemaster*: 'It is a marvellous pain to find out a short way by long wandering.' The one gain of learning the art of preaching is that it may save us from this 'long wandering'! In the end, of course, our finest teacher will be practice. I venture to say that you will learn more in your first three months as a minister than I or any one else can ever tell you. And perhaps, if you are men of open mind, your failures will be your finest tutor.

3. WHAT IS PREACHING?

To us, preaching is the natural overflow of our religion. We have received good news, and we long to tell it to others. Our religion is like joy we cannot suppress or contain. It bubbles over like a brimming cup. The reason and passion of preaching—the only reason and passion—is that a great and wonderful thing has come into our own lives in the love of God through Jesus, and we can find no rest until we tell the world. Preaching is not a duty in any sense, but a sheer, inevitable joy. It is a spontaneous passion, like the coming of love into a young man's heart: and unless it has some of that joy and passion in it for you, I pity you ten years hence! God has shown us His full love, and that love is a contagion. If this is not somehow in our hearts, our preaching is either a performance, interesting and clever, or a mere office, or worst of all, a subtle type of insincerity. To preach without reality and passion may do no lasting mischief to a congregation: but in the end, it will blight our own spiritual life like a plague. The man who suffers most by any type of hypocrisy is the hypocrite himself.

In its simplest and most diluted form, preaching is telling someone else about Jesus Christ, and opening out the mind and will of God. Its idea is to spread the news, convince others, and lead them to the same peace and joy as we possess. This dictates the two forms which preaching generally assumes: on the one hand, to convince the careless, awaken the indifferent, and enlighten the ignorant, in other words, to make converts, here or abroad, conversion through conviction; and on the other hand, to educate, train, nourish and inspire those who are already convinced, to upbuild and strengthen the people of God. In some of the books which it has been my mingled pleasure and pain to read, I have found it debated at great length which of these two ideas of preaching is more fundamental and necessary. But in any effective preaching are they ever separate? They are woven together like the warp and the woof. Whether preaching is to convert or to instruct? Why, often before you can instruct you must convert, and often before you can convert, you must instruct. And even in a settled congregation, among admittedly Christian people, the harmony between the two need never be broken. I do not know any congregation where there are not people to be awakened, sometimes startled and shocked: and I do not know any congregation where there are not people to be instructed.

The purpose and aim of preaching then, however we subdivide it, is to bring men and women to God. It is to present Jesus as the fullness of our life, the Lord and Saviour, and His religion as the fine crown of things. This may take many forms, rebuke or inspiration, warning or comfort, teaching or exhortation. Generally, the rounder and more varied your preaching is, in matter and method alike, the better the work, and the richer the results.

THE DIFFICULTIES OF MODERN PREACHING

'To bring men and women to God.' How can this be done to-day, amid the special circumstances of our age? Before we consider what preaching is or the qualities that go to make its strength or weakness, I think we ought to discuss the situation in which we as preachers are placed. Can we hope to do the work our predecessors did so nobly in past days? Has the pulpit a future?

No man of any outlook can help noticing the silent changes that have taken place within recent times, which must exercise an influence both on the matter and method of our work. We have no right to 'play the ostrich', shutting our eyes to these changes, and preaching as if they had never taken place; for in the best sense, every man of any mettle must speak to his own age and adjust himself to its peculiar problems.

I. THE SPIRIT OF REBELLION

Among these changes I note first, because it is most intrusive, the modern revolt against authority. This revolt is not peculiar to religion alone, for it is a symptom of the age. Some might call it a disease of the age: but that depends on our outlook, sometimes on our politics! In religion especially, this revolt affects the creed of the Church, the recognition of the Bible, the standing of the minister, and the acceptance of his message. We have lost to-day the old type of authority when the decrees of the Church were as the laws of the Crown. A minister's word is not received to-day, as formerly, because he is, or thinks he is, a priest and an oracle of God. Nor are views accepted because they are stated in the Bible. The Book itself is under the searchlight. But I don't fear the searchlight. The truth should bear all scrutiny. As compared with past days, our calling has suffered in the prestige of authority.

I said 'suffered'. But have we suffered? Frankly, I do not regret the passing of all types of merely external authority. Men are thinking to-day, and are free to think. I believe that the Christian religion is safe so long, and only so long, as men remain thinking. It is not thought but want of thought that empties our churches. If only we get people to think—about themselves, about life and its values, about duty and destiny, about God and the soul—we need have little fear. Thought only drives a man back among the mysteries, and amid these he finds the greatest of all, the one that solves them all, God. And for a man to face God is the beginning of things. Any form of religion which discourages or suppresses thought will itself be suppressed. It is really no loss to us or religion that men cannot be any longer commanded or herded. The day for that—religion as a majestic drum-major or drill-sergeant—is happily past. Nor is it a loss that people no longer come to church from custom or decency or social respect. The Church is really stronger when it has fewer camp-followers or passengers, who hang on to it, not from love or need, but for the occasional use of a minister's services. A hundred convinced people are likely to do more for Christ and the world than a thousand who are slack and dilute enthusiasm into apathy.

But we have a far finer authority than any we have forfeited. We have the authority of truth itself, the only authority the Apostles ever had, and the one thing that gave them their passionate and prophetic note. They spoke in the name of God and righteousness, and the big needs of the human soul. With the love of Jesus, the world's Redeemer, in their hearts, they turned that world upside down. If you and I can only recapture their love for Jesus and their persuasion that men need Christ, we too shall do apostolic work. The best authority lies in passionate conviction and in love.

2. THE PLACE OF FEAR

We have lost also the ancient authority of fear. What an immense armoury the old preachers had, when they could almost invoke the licking flames of hell! Have we really lost by this loss? Is it better to woo men or drive them? Mark you, however, there is still a place for healthy fear. We have stopped preaching fear in the pulpit: and now our doctors and our scientists have taken it up. I do not know anybody who preaches punishment more unflinchingly to-day than an honest doctor or a scientist expounding laws. They show that the breach of physical law entails the lash. You can almost hear the cracking whip as they speak. But we have become 'mealy-mouthed' in speaking about punishment. Punishment! Why! the whole creation is grim with it. It is the one religious doctrine that has been buttressed by every discovery. 'Whoso breaketh an hedge, a serpent shall bite him.' Use fear, gentlemen, healthy fear: and preach 'sin'. Sin in its protean forms is the world's big fact. It is so big that it takes a Cross with a Christ to measure it. You will never save a man by making his sin a casual thing, something a little regrettable, or as an ordinary process through which, by experiment, a man climbs to higher things, a thin gospel of 'good in the making'—mankind falling upwards. That may be fashionable to-day, but its condemnation lies in the fact that it leaves the world untouched and unredeemed. If we are in any sense followers of Jesus, the note that sin is not neutral but is flaming scarlet must run through our message. So also with the clear call to repentance. 'Repent ye and believe the Gospel.' You can have any views you like about the after-life, or about punishment, but you cannot miss this, that Jesus said some plain and terrible things about those who do not repent.

Still we are wise not to drive with fear, but win with love. I do not think we have lost in this exchange. It is a far finer thing to win a man by the vision of the King in His beauty, by the love of God, and the attraction of Jesus. That holds when other links snap.

3. THE ACID TEST OF CRITICISM

We have no prepared audience to-day. In times not too distant, a minister might count on a people with some knowledge of the Bible and a certain interest in theology. This was especially true of my own heather hills in Scotland, where the ancient argumentative faculty of our people found full scope in discussing theological questions, with the appetite of a dog for a meaty bone: and I presume this was true of America, wherever the Puritan strain ran deepest.

Instead of this there is a critical attitude to the Church and religion. Indeed, it is a kind of sneer nowadays to say that a man has an 'ecclesiastical mind', as if that were something full of pedantries and hedging quirks, and as if such a mind were always trying to compromise contradictories. The criticism of the Church extends to its creed, which in form and matter is said to be hopelessly out-of-date, like some of our Scottish castles—a noble ruin, but a ruin.

Even the moral teaching of the Church is not without its biting criticism. Some people, while admiring it, question if it is practicable in modern life and business. Nietzsche dubbed it openly a 'slave morality', and preached as a substitute what he called the religion of the super-man. And although in these last few years the religion of the super-man has been shown to be red ruin, the law of the claw and the talon, the jungle let loose, still the criticism has done damage. For if you only throw enough mud in this world, some of it is sure to stick.

Moreover, apart from this semi-philosophical criticism, there is the popular estimate that the moral outlook of religion narrows and stifles life, robs it of any spontaneous natural joy, cribs and cabins our manhood, and manufactures a type of sainthood that is a distortion, if not a disease. Swinburne, you remember, laments that the narrow spirit of Jesus came like a blight over the joyous mind of Greece, and chased laughter and music out of the world, to replace it by the drab decencies and prudish righteousness of the priest and the puritan.

> Thou hast conquered, O pale Galilean: the world has grown gray from Thy breath;
> We have drunken of things Lethean, and fed on the fullness of death.

Now, all this atmosphere of criticism may seem a hindrance to our work, but in reality it is an aid. Personally, I would rather speak to a man who thinks, even if he rejects, than to a man who accepts without thinking. We have thereby the gain of a moving, not a somnolent world: we have an enquiring and questioning audience: we have people everywhere restless and disturbed, and seeking guidance and peace of mind. In view of this, as preachers, we are faced with a unique opportunity. Ours is a great vocation, just to have the privilege of addressing an age like this. The gasping fashion in which people adopt fancy religions or potter after 'chirping' spiritualism is, if we understand it rightly, one of the big notes of hope in our age. It shows that men are needing, consciously needing, something a little bigger than themselves and are searching for a message of truth. It is a hungry world.

4. DOES JESUS NARROW LIFE?

In face of all this we have to be sure of three things.

(*a*) We have to show that Christianity is not against the natural life, as Swinburne claimed, but is simply the natural life purified, refined and perfected in God. The Puritan movement was a glorious crusade that cleansed and sweetened this old world: but in the by-going it did us a grave disservice in splitting life into sacred and secular, and giving all the fun and laughter apparently to the secular. Whatever was natural and joyous, was evil. Laughter was the proof of a careless soul! A man could only serve God in long-faced solemnity and sacrifice! No wonder, in misconception, the modern man thinks that Christ beggars and robs human life. It is our duty to show that Christianity is just human life, in all its bigness and width, in all its wonder and sweep, raised to the 'nth power', glorified, sweetened, purified and enlarged. If there is any super-man at all, it is the Christian man.

(*b*) We have to prove that Christianity *can be lived*, simply by living it. Its demands are high, a fact which is not our regret but our boast. That its moral claims are hard to fulfil in this world is not a condemnation of it but of the world. We have to show that Christianity is not a string of rules and requirements, difficult to harmonise, a reformed Judaism, but that its regulative principle is Christ's law of love. And we have to show that this law of love is the big solvent for the puzzles of private life, for business, for pleasure, and for the hate and passion of the world. If that law of love is not lived, by men and nations alike, then I foresee nothing but a re-emergence of the jungle.

(*c*) And as to the charge that the Church has been an obstacle to progress, we had better frankly admit the partial truth: partial in this sense, that as an institution, like all other institutions, the Church has tended to favour the status quo. In time, all organisations, even organisations for progress, tend to become conservative, fearing new things. And the Church has not been without its guilt, for having a fixed doctrine, it has tended to have a fixed outlook. But partial also in this sense, that every great movement of progress has had the passion and pity of Jesus Christ as its origin and inspiration, and has always appealed for support to the mind of Jesus. Even some extreme forms of socialism and communism, often anti-Church, are seldom anti-Jesus. They actually 'quote' Jesus against the Church, using Him as a test of truth.

5. FAITH IN THE MELTING-POT

We labour to-day under the disadvantage that so many of our

ancient statements and formulations of faith are in the melting-pot. Now, I do not fear the melting-pot. For in the melting-pot the nature of any material is never changed, though its *form* may be. Perhaps we may need change of form or at least change of definition. The second century cannot be expected to speak for the twentieth, and the East cannot be expected to think in the modes of the West. You Americans especially, with your gift for nervous phrasing, have claimed the right to speak in your own virile modern tongue, and define our common faith in terms of your own genius. I do not question this natural right. But all this need not affect the substance of true faith. We can define Jesus to-day as Redeemer, Lord, and Son, without being bound to the obscure notions of the Greek Gnostics and Platonists. Indeed, just as the thinkers of the first century expressed their faith in the terms of their own day, it is incumbent on us to express it in the terms of our day. The genius of all good writing is that it translates ancient phrases into the speech and categories of its own time. But beyond this, the fault of our early creeds was that their framers attempted to define the indefinable, and crush Jesus and God into a phrase. Jesus and God may remain the same, but the phrase, like old clothes, may need some tailoring. I think it is incumbent on us, soon, to express our faith in more modern language. Meanwhile, people ask us what they are to believe, when we ourselves as ministers claim the privilege of 'Declaratory Acts' to give us liberty from the bondage of ancient phrases. It is not right for us to lock the front door, and slip out by the back ourselves.

I have tried to indicate a few of the changed conditions under which we must conduct our ministry. If they are puzzling, they only call for the greater courage and consecration on our part that we may exhibit Jesus as the one way in which the world can be touched. I said the 'one way'. Nothing becomes clearer than that, the more of other expedients we try. 'How to redeem this broken old world?' Like many of you, I have favoured all sorts of schemes for its salvation, and I have found them invariably good but woefully insufficient. For what we need is not merely salvation from circumstances, or salvation from environment, or salvation from others, but salvation from ourselves, from the sin we have and the sin we are. 'There is none other name under heaven given among men whereby we must be saved.'

OUR GROUNDS FOR HOPE

I have spoken of difficulties. May I speak, as I close, about some encouraging symptoms peculiar to our own age, the note of the lark that augurs the new greenness of growth?

I. THE SEARCH FOR REST

The clearest note of hope lies in the very heart of man that is restlessly seeking rest. There never was an age so sure of insecurity. We have seen things hoary with age and respect smashed to dust before our eyes. We talked with fatuous smiles about the doctrines of 'humanity' and the creed of 'civilisation', as if we could be saved by abstractions! We coined fine phrases and generalisations, and trusted that they represented real things, some magic power that would police the world's passions. But we have seen these abstractions, in the face of aggressive hate and greed, proved a lying myth. Not only kingdoms have crumbled, but worse, ideas also: and what we vainly call 'rights' have toppled with them. And many dazed souls have wondered if there remained anything sure or permanent that could demand respect or veneration.

More than this, there have been so many hearts and homes bleached white with loss, that millions of people to-day would sell their souls just to know the fate of those whom they loved and lost. And they, unbuttressed by any true religion, are turning to fancy faiths and quirky mediums, gasping for an assurance that only the love of God in Jesus can ever provide. In all this, while we lament the ignorance that turns them into blind alleys, there is a great outlook for a true faith, a prepared court of hearing. People, more now than ever, are open to see the mystery of life, no longer shut and sealed with petty dogmatisms. Men have been taken out into the endless wastes of the world, and their eyes are dark with shadowing mystery. Life is no longer the little facile thing it was, belittled by our smug complacencies. But it has meanings and reaches and possibilities, even if only of suffering, that were undreamt of in the last generation.

Where tides meet, there is broken water. We have been swept on the tides, and are living now on the back-wash. No doubt, it is an age of unsettlement. What else could one expect? But an age of unsettlement may be, and generally has been, the prelude to an age of faith. Meanwhile, people are asking for direction, like wandering men on a heath. We claim to have the living way. Can we show it? If we can, making life big, and revealing its eternal values and its worth in Jesus, we shall have before us a ring of expectant faces.

2. ROOM FOR JESUS

Both in practical life and in philosophy, the grip of materialism is broken. This has been particularly noticeable in philosophical thinking, where recent writers of distinction have been veering round to vitalistic and idealistic and even Christian conclusions. The atmosphere of thought has never been more favourable to a spiritual outlook than it is to-day, although for the concerns of real religion I should not lay too much stress on the help of 'neutral allies'. But it is worth observing that philosophers and scientists regard man as less of a material thing and more of a spiritual being, not a machine but a soul, whose greatness lies not in his likeness to the world but in his difference from it and in his command of it, and whose explanation consists not in any suggested origins but in his destinies and in his dreams. We do not find reputable people nowadays presuming to sum up man in an epigram or in terms of the savage or the gorilla. We no longer think that we can explain creation simply by describing processes: and evolution, even if it were all true, only pushes the mystery further back. We even recognise now that what we call the laws of nature, formerly a scientific fetish, are simply working hypotheses, 'conjectures on trial', something which meanwhile conveniently explains the scanty facts observed, but which may be ruthlessly scrapped as soon as fresh knowledge shows that they do not work.

All this is very enlarging from our point of view. It gives fresh point to the old remark in *Hamlet*,

> There are more things in heaven and earth, Horatio,
> Than are dreamt of in your philosophy.

It frankly confesses the unknown and the unknowable, so that the confident generalisations of Herbert Spencer and the crudisms of Haeckel are as dead as Queen Anne. Philosophy and science at least recognise that there is room for other explanations, and religion is not discounted before it is heard.

3. THE CHURCH'S CLAIM ON LIFE

The Church itself, by its own sane development, has ruled out the paganism of Swinburne on the one hand, and the secularist crusade of Bradlaugh and Holyoake on the other.

(*a*) Christianity has made its great claim to the joy and youth of life, as against Swinburne's sonorous nonsense. We have learned in the first place that the Greek spirit was not all 'joy', but was one of the darkest things that blighted the human outlook. If there was laughter, it was the crackling laughter of carelessness. But in reality Greek thought was dogged by tragedy. There is nothing just so unmeaningly dark as the Greek dramas in their exposition of fate and the crooked will of things. They are the parents of fatalism, stern and unrelieved. The Stoic creed itself, with its doctrine of 'indifference', is just a sublimated form of fatalism, a will to make the best of things amid the mysteries of conduct and thought. The Greek people are like a group of children standing in a glowing patch of sunshine, with engrossing mists around. Those who were concerned only with the present, or who were blessed with youth's red blood, cried, 'How lovely is the sunshine! let us dance and sing.' But those who exercised the dreaming prerogative of man saw chiefly the mists, the agony of which was heightened by the glaring patch of sunshine. If you want to hear the pattering feet of the dogs of fate, read Greek literature. Then speak to me of its light-hearted gaiety. Some gaiety was there, but what was its moral value? It was there, not in the heart of the thinker, but in the heart of the thoughtless, and there only so long as the sunshine lasted.

(*b*) But further, the Church, outgrowing its own sober tendencies and seeing its message in its natural fullness, has claimed all life for Jesus—youth, joy, the laughter of little children, the gospel of the beautiful, the love of music and art, the sacred and the secular alike, without distinction. After some expensive mistakes and many defaming limitations of the mind of Jesus, it has learned that the only pleasures that are evil are evil pleasures; that man was made to sing as well as sigh; and that life is consecrated not only by great refusals but also by great acceptances. And so the Christian life, above all other types, is the life that is lived in sunshine, the sunshine of the smile of God. It is the natural life, cleansed and then crowned.

(*c*) And on the other hand, as against the just charges of

Bradlaugh and Holyoake and their more recent exponents, the Church has learned that it must concern itself not only with the dreamy glories of heaven but also with the real miseries of earth, and with the body as with the soul of man. No effective Church but must have its social programme, a changed man in a changed world—the one as needful as the other. With this in our heart, the just satires of the secularism of yesterday are cleansed of their venom.

4. A LONELY FIGURE UNASSAILED

The greatest note of hopefulness for our message is one which I, with others, discovered in the armed forces. There I met with a refreshing criticism of the Church as an institution, often biased and short-sighted, sometimes a cloak of excuse for personal indifference, not infrequently jaundiced by social views which the speaker foolishly considered hostile, but always frank and pithily expressed. It is fair to admit that much of this hostility is justly earned, for the Church has often seemed to side with the powers that be, and fools robed in cassocks have counselled contentment when they should have urged rebellion and a divine discontent. But amid all this criticism of the Church, I have never met anyone who criticised its Lord. Indeed, the main charge of such critics was that the Church, professing Him, was so unlike Him. I was astonished to find, even when they belonged to no church, how much our soldiers knew of Christ's practical message for the world, and how much they reverenced Him for it. They might criticise us, but they never criticised Him. And the moral is, that the nearer we get to Him, the nearer shall we get to the world.

To-day, as I close, I should like you to see that in a world of need and passion, there stands, unblemished and unassailed, the figure of Jesus, whose love has softened the hearts of men and whose purity has hushed their clamour. If we preach Jesus the Saviour, in the majesty both of His goodness and His pity, I prophesy a listening world.

And what more does a preacher want?

2 A Preacher's Requisites

I venerate the man whose heart is warm,
Whose hands are pure, whose doctrine and whose life,
Coincident, exhibit lucid proof
That he is honest in the sacred cause.

WILLIAM COWPER, *The Task*, Book II

Preaching presupposes three things: an audience, a message, and a preacher.

PREACHING PRESUPPOSES AN AUDIENCE

Since it is a public thing, spoken and delivered, it presupposes an audience. Unfortunately, in a double sense, that may be the one thing we cannot guarantee. But behind all preaching, during our preparation in the study or in the execution itself, there should be *the shadow of a listening people*. To forget that is the next crime to forgetting God.

I begin with this because it is the most regulative thing in the sermon. The form, tone, and colour of preaching are definitely prescribed by this fact. Were it otherwise, the sermon might easily assume another guise. It might be an essay, a pamphlet, an article, or what we loosely call 'a paper'. Incidentally the failure of many sermons, as preached, is that they have little or no relation to the audience, and are practically essays. They may furnish an excellent treatment of their subject, accurate, full and balanced, but they might as well be privately printed and privately read. It is the ideal of a message spoken from one heart to another that gives the sermon its distinctive form; and behind it, even as it stands in the 'stocks' in a man's study, is this shadow of a listening people. In this connection, someone has said that a good sermon, as preached, never reads well, and never should.

You are going, I trust, to speak to people, not benches, and especially to people hearing, not reading. This latter fact speaks volumes to a wise man. The idea that he is speaking to listening people will affect his treatment, method, language, and policy. When we are reading, we have ample opportunity of going at our own set pace. We can halt to reflect on certain aspects and statements, or we can amble back at leisure and relate one thing to another. But in public speech, a hearer has no such golden opportunities. If he misses a plank in the argument, he must simply step over the gap as best he can. A wise speaker, remembering this, will avoid typical 'literary' speech, with involved forms and evasive allusions. He will prune his language of all over-refinements and puzzling cleverness. If need be, he may even deal in judicious repetition. He will effect some simplification of matter and structure; for his object, if he would move his audience, is to be immediately understood. It is disastrous for him if people have to worry out obscure meanings and hold their breath during involved and tousled sentences.

Further, since we are speaking to people, we must know the big common heart of those we address. If there are great differences between people, there are greater likenesses. At first we might think that a knowledge of our own heart would enable us to speak with success to the hearts of others. Yet I have known some finely introspective preachers and analytical writers who have made little appeal to others, except to the select few, people of their own kidney. Above all self-knowledge, we must know the work and conditions, the pastimes and pleasures, the ideals and dreams, the temptations and the tangled motives of the people we address. Incidentally, that is why no preacher, however great, can afford to do without the intimate human knowledge which he acquires by visiting. Otherwise, he ends by addressing an audience and not a congregation, the soul of man and not souls. And what is the 'soul of man' but a polite abstraction?

For this purpose we must be as interested in people as in ideas. The secret of men like Walter Scott and Charles Dickens lay in the fact that they had the 'key of the street'. They knew the ordinary man and woman of the city street and the hillside, humanity in its health and disease, in its motives, passions and temptations, in its laughter and tears, and in the joy of big clean simple things. Above all, they knew the clutch of habit, the creaky working of the human will, and the glorious response of a man's soul. This gave them a mingled gentleness and severity, akin to the gentleness and severity of God, who knows us through and through and therefore understands. The root of any healing sympathy, human or divine, is knowledge of human nature.

I. THE SENSE OF AN AUDIENCE

Following this out, I believe that we do not sufficiently train our young ministers to what I call 'the sense of an audience', the one thing that will determine the form of our future work. Every other aspect of our preparation is minutely finished. No finer training for the 'material' of our preaching can be had than you have here in your colleges. But generally—I speak from my own experience—a young man, when 'finished', is sent out to a luckless congregation with everything in the art of speech to learn, generally by crude experiment on a long-suffering people. I am afraid the fault lies with our college curriculum. We do not treat the training in the art of speech with sufficient respect and courtesy. Indeed, some of our good professors regard the subject as a little beneath the dignity of the college, and as contributing mainly to flashy and meretricious arts. A stray hour now and then—as we had it, in our final year—is not enough for a class of speech-training. After all, the one thing a man has to do in his professional life is to *speak*, and to speak often to an audience where there are countless trained speakers. What chance will his message have—for persuasion, for drive, for power, for conviction—if he has no sufficient training in effective deliverance? The average student—I am speaking here of what I know best, our own colleges in Scotland—does not lack 'matter' or a fine knowledge of his subject: but he *does* lack the art of presentation and the technique of preaching. And quite often—a more ruinous loss—he lacks any saving and controlling idea of the theory of worship.

I am not narrowing this down to mere speaking or utterance. There are a hundred other things along this line that can be helpfully taught and learned. There is, for instance, some knowledge of the psychology of an audience. It is not enough to know how to treat our subject, if we do not know how to treat our people. As I have listened to great speakers, distinctive speakers, it is not only how they handle their subjects that marks them off from others, but how they handle their audience and themselves. They know how and when to appeal, how to use legitimate emotion, how to build up an argument, how to illustrate obscure points, how to plan the architecture of their material, how to gain a verdict, how to be restrained, how even to 'rest' their people in the progress of their argument. They are masters of themselves as well as of their subjects.

You say, no doubt, that this is only learned by practice, and even then some people will never learn it. I agree. The real speaker is born—but he is also made. And when you think that all our effectiveness in after days will depend on our utterance, don't you agree that it is not enough to trust to a kindly but overworked providence, and a young man's chance experience in a country church? I am astonished at the effectiveness of the average American preacher: and I venture to say that if he had the same grounding and mental foundation as you have here in this school of training, he would be a wonderful product. But the reason is—preachers are really trained in America!

PREACHING PRESUPPOSES A MESSAGE

For all true purposes the message is central. Everything I have said, or have yet to say, is wholly subsidiary to this. The value of everything else is that it may contribute to the effectiveness of the message, may help or hinder it.

This is the one thing you and I have to make sure of—that we do not merely say something because with the round of the week the time for saying it has come, but that we have something to say, a definite message laid on our own hearts, what the prophets called a 'Burden'.

It would be idle for me to use time in speaking to you of the content of that message. Perhaps it might even seem a little presuming and impertinent. The fact that you are here in this college studying for the office of the ministry shows that you have been apprehended of Christ, and that your dream is to be a servant and channel of His grace.

But I may be allowed to speak of one or two things in this connection, even though I should refer to them later.

I. THE BIG TRUTHS

In delivering your message, *keep near to the big controlling truths.*

Most of us are assailed now and then by the desire to be fanciful or original, and we ferret out sensational subjects and deal in side lines. The danger of this is that it is apt to be cheap: and the man who lives on thrills and startling subjects becomes a bit of a mountebank. Worst of all—for no man can keep it up—he becomes 'panned out', and the end of that man is a spent squib!

But originality, so precious to our vain souls, need never be repressed, for it has full scope to display itself in a fresh and original treatment of the big facts of our faith. In any case, you will notice in a few years that these big truths, as crystallised perhaps in a rich and sappy text, have a swing and volume, a natural 'carry' of their own, the effect of which is marvellous to observe in the eyes of a congregation.

The big subjects often do their own work, with or without us, perhaps even in spite of us.

Moreover, it is a failure of duty if we neglect to deal with the truths that are presumably meat to our own soul. If this or that is the axis of our own life, it ought to be the axis of our message. Religion for us inevitably suggests Jesus. It is difficult to think of Jesus without thinking of a cross. The Cross speaks of a world gone wrong, and a world redeemed. And for the follower of Christ there is the life of mingled demand and glory, of gain through loss. If this be the heart of us, should it not be the heart of our message? Preach on issues, not on side-issues. The world is needy and there are countless souls who come up to church every Sunday praying for comfort and direction, as lost men. To offer them a string of cheap epigrams or bloodless moralities is to feed them on stones. I fear nothing so much as the 'clever' minister! Amid all life's agonies and sorrows, he is not only a tragic misfit but also a cruel irony.

It is the big truths that heal—and it is *healing* that men need. When I think sometimes of the puzzled and burdened hearts in every congregation, whose hurt perhaps is concealed under a twisted smile: business men and women who are worried equally by the problems of failure or success: young men and women bravely fighting the rising passion of their own blood and tempted to risk everything on some wild throw: people with inarticulate prayers for the life or soul of some loved one: a home with a great big hole in it that nothing human can ever fill: nameless sorrows that tears can never ease, and people who keep living though they have nothing left to live for: memories that are just one longing ache, or those that bite like venom—when I remember all this, I cannot but think that some of our smart and flashy sermons are as thoughtlessly cruel as they are impertinent.

Get deep down, deep down. You may hurt, but you will heal. Handle in God's love the big gracious things that can alone give courage, comfort, and hope to the unknown seekers who may never thank you except in their prayers.

2. YOUR OWN OR YOUR FATHER'S RELIGION

That leads me to my second remark—*preach nothing other than you believe.* Borrowed beliefs have no power: they are ineffectual angels. What you yourself have proved and what is bone of your bone, has an almost electric power on people, and will certainly have an electric power on you. Coleridge remarks in his *Aids to Reflection* that 'truth needs not the service of passion'. That is one of the neat aphorisms that fascinated Coleridge's type of mind, but like most epigrams, it is a half lie. If there is anything that creates a peculiar passion, it is truth. It generates its own white heat. And if you preach what you believe, as if you believed it, as if it meant everything to you, there will be a natural ring and passion in your word that is infinitely better than any extraneous type of eloquence.

In this connection I have heard it said that the truth should be quietly and soberly delivered, and should be allowed to do its own gracious work. But have you ever known anybody, outside the pulpit, who was quiet and sober about truth? Truth is the one thing in every age and station that has set the heather on fire. It has led martyrs to the stake with shining eyes, and turned the world upside down. I can't understand a man, speaking of a topic that concerns his own soul and the salvation of man, preaching with casualness or insipidity. If only he is in earnest and speaks as he believes, there will be a ring even in his voice that will command and arrest. Please do not be ashamed of the enthusiasm that truth generates. All the great ages of history have been ages of enthusiasm, drunk with dreams. It was sheer enthusiasm that built and held the early Church, the passion of high belief, truth held so dear that as compared with it life was cheap.

There is a little-known tale about Hume, the philosopher, which may illustrate my point. It was told me by the grand-daughter of the minister who figures in the story. Hume, as you may guess, seldom entered a church-door. But when he paid an annual visit to Haddingtonshire, he invariably attended the little Scottish church in the village. Some of the wits who were staying with him at the country-house accompanied him one Sunday, from curiosity, to see what could possibly attract the great sceptic. They heard what seemed to them an uninteresting monologue on an outworn creed, through which at first they yawned, and afterwards played dice. When the service was over, they quizzed Hume about his sudden conversion to church ways. Hume turned on them rather fiercely and answered, 'That old man believed every word he uttered!' Dr. Walter Lingle, Professor of Church History at Union Seminary, Richmond, relates a similar tale about Hume. Dr. Lingle writes: It is related that a friend one day met David Hume, the historian and philosopher, hurrying along the streets of London, and asked him where he was going. Hume replied that he was going to hear George Whitefield preach. The friend, remembering that Hume was none too friendly to Christianity, said, 'Surely you do not believe what Whitefield is preaching, do you?' 'No,' replied Hume, 'but he does.'

Preach only what you believe. It is the one type of preaching with magic in it. If you only know about sin, *preach sin.* If you only know about punishment, *preach punishment.* If you only know about sorrow and comfort, *preach sorrow and comfort.* If you only know about grace and forgiveness, *preach grace and forgiveness.* Only what is real to you can be real to anybody else. But mark you, while I say 'Preach what you believe', I do not suggest for one moment that you should preach only your own pet views and cranky theories. If the full faith is ours, it is our privilege to preach it in roundness and variety. But naturally, there are aspects of the faith to which only experience can serve us heirs, aspects into which we can only enter in the ripeness of years, sometimes in the ripeness of sorrow and unbelievable loss. I do not think that you are called upon to preach doctrines you have not yet made your own. You cannot live on your father's religion, or even the Church's catholic religion, but on your own religion. In other words, you cannot preach on a subject just because other people expect you to preach on it. Strive, if possible, to enter into the full and rich faith—and it is a strength in preaching to remember that it has been the tested faith of generations—but until you can do that, preach what you believe. The one sure note of power is *sincerity.* If that is absent, preaching is only a noise. If it is there, it may atone for every other omission among honest hearts.

3. PREACHING WITH INTEREST

Try to preach with interest. I mentioned in my opening lecture that some of my correspondents preferred 'interest' in a sermon to anything else. But one may well ask, what is interest? May I try to work out with you some of the elements which may constitute or compel interest?

(*a*) Interest may lie first of all in the subject you choose. However, you should have enough human knowledge—'gumption' we call it in Scotland—to know that what may be fascinating to you as students may be as dull as ditch-water to any ordinary congregation. A scientist may be immensely interested in the conservation of energy or in a theory of electrons, but both of these subjects are likely to bore the average man to tears. And you, as Bible students, may be fascinated by certain scholarly problems or philosophical considerations, which will only float like drifting clouds over your people's heads. Therefore you ought to have enough 'gumption' to know that what interests you is not the unfailing test.

But if the subject you choose has a broad 'human' interest, touching the daily concerns and questions of our common humanity, it is likely to be arresting, or at least of general appeal. You can almost picture a man nodding his head, as if to say, 'Why, yes! that has often puzzled me, and I would value some guidance.' Life is crammed with common problems—our sin is that we don't see how general they are—difficulties, troubles, passions, temptations and sins. It is like an April day, chequered by alternate laughter and tears. If your own life is so placed that you cannot 'glimpse' these problems for yourself, I should invite people, if I were you, to suggest subjects for your sermons. But, in that case, I fear the danger may be that you would treat them only *ex cathedra* and without understanding sympathy: and this being so, it might be better to leave them alone! But if you have any experience of sin and sorrow, of drenching repentance and the grace of God, you will easily get into touch with the great questions of the human heart.

Generally, unless we are dull dogs, it is a revelation to observe the interest of an audience when we deal with the common experiences of men and women. They can 'go with us', corroborate or check us in our inferences, and respond to appeals that express their own undefined longings. Try to help and guide your people in the problems of their tangled life, and show them the great way out. Such preaching is of perennial interest.

On this point it is good to remember that interest, at any time, depends on the attention being arrested. Unfortunately, very few people are trained to attend. But if a subject grips them straightaway, the rest depends on you. In this particular, remember that even the best hearers cannot attend without a break for any length of time. Whether this fact should affect the duration of your sermon is for you to say. In any case, you should have means for 'resting' an audience, and then gripping them up again. It is said that Gladstone had periods in his addresses where it did not matter much whether people listened or not. He was *resting* them. Others do this with a relevant anecdote or illustration. Then, when they resume their discussion or argument, they grip the people afresh. One use of divisions in our sermon, or at least in our thought, is that they provide these 'easing-off' places naturally and yet artistically. But fine skill is needed lest the easing off be too thorough, and the break too complete. You must never fish with too much 'slack'!

I stress this point again—choose subjects of general interest to your people and get down to the business of living. There is no difficulty in getting an audience to listen at a big political meeting. The reason is simple—the subject is in everybody's mind. Can we not touch the common heart more than we do? You will find that the sermons that help are those that have played upon the heart-strings, though at the time they may have hurt.

(*b*) Interest depends not only on your subject, but also on your treatment of it. A lively treatment can often invest a dull subject with glamour; whereas a heavy manner may swamp a big topic in dullness. Psychology and astronomy, in themselves, are not enlivening subjects for the average man: but the manner in which William James of Harvard treated the former and Sir Robert Ball dealt with the latter, is a revelation in the science of treatment. On the other hand, the *Rasselas* of Samuel Johnson is a classic instance of how a ponderous manner and treatment may strangle a big idea or ruin a fine situation. Imagine Defoe or H. G. Wells handling the 'happy valley' of Rasselas!

For interest of treatment, we should study the best methods of modern teaching. This will show us how to handle our material, and help us towards a lively, vigorous statement of it. As you may have often noticed, two speakers will deal with the same topic and material in two quite different ways: and it is this *difference of treatment* rather than of matter that may make one of them brilliant and the other prosy. As a general rule, try to catch the interest of your people in the first five minutes, perhaps by some arresting way of putting things. If you don't grip them in the first five minutes, you haven't much chance afterwards!

That our treatment of material means much is shown in all the great writers. Some unthinking critics say that Shakespeare and Scott only cribbed their plots and stories from earlier sources. Perhaps they did. But in the best sense, this was no piracy: for everything that is eternal in Scott and Shakespeare is—Scott and Shakespeare! It is their distinct treatment of some old common story of the hedge-side and the lanes, that makes them world-masters. It has been proved that Defoe freely used an earlier Dutch source for his story of Robinson Crusoe. But amid all the similarities of situation and incident, there is genius in the one and only merit in the other. Robert Burns, quite openly, appropriated his rhymes and melodies from the immemorial folk-songs of the Scottish countryside: but his treatment of these old songs and tunes only emphasises his particular genius. Edgar Rice Burroughs has written some striking tales about Tarzan, who lived with the apes. But all through his books I have caught myself saying, 'if only the idea had occurred to Rudyard Kipling!' The man who made Mowgli would have made Tarzan immortal. There is not so much difference in *matter* between writers and speakers: genius shows itself in treatment.

As far as methods of treatment go, first try to get your subject into its own compass—seeing it as a whole and seeing it as a *power*—with a real beginning and a real end. Let its natural development and progress be quite clear, so that people feel its movement as if it were a thing of life, as one feels the pulse of the blood. Let it rise, in this fine progress, to its suitable and indeed inevitable climax. Don't be tempted to over-elaborate parts or passing points, for that is a fault of balance—and even a kind of slur on your people's intelligence. Then consider how you may lighten or illustrate your ideas. Where possible, use some imaginative treatment.

(All the great preachers—I don't say all the great sermon-writers—have been imaginative.) In regard to language, be short and terse, forming your sentences in simple construction. Dull, laboured and tangled sentences, with bedraggled dependent clauses, are more responsible for 'heaviness' than any other item in preaching. However, I hope to stress some of these points in my next lecture.

(*c*) The third source of interest is the man himself, whatever is distinctive and arresting in his personality. Some people have gifts of presence, face, voice and style that immediately help to win or at least interest an audience. But while these may be desirable, unless they are backed up by bigger things, they count as so much froth. Indeed, after a time, they may only prejudice an audience unfavourably. As with the 'green fig tree', which promised more than it could fulfil, the people may end by blasting the man.

Personality betrays itself mainly in original points of view, or in distinctive turns of thought, or in arresting forms of expression, or in typical mannerisms. 'Thy speech bewrayeth thee,' and should bewray thee. The question is, should these qualities, or can these qualities, be cultivated wisely? Or should we try to conform to a common decency? Personality is such a priceless thing, in any sphere of life, that there is only one answer. Be as distinctive as you can, so long as you are not angular: and use your own methods, so long as you are not gauche or rude. Meanwhile I refer you to a later part of this lecture where I stress this subject in a more fitting context.

4. PREACHING AS A MODERN MAN

That leads me to my next point—*preach in modern ways.* This does not refer only to fashions and methods and expressions. That of course is imperative. In the best sense, every man must be the servant of his age and speak through its accepted modes of thought. But more than that, preach in the peculiar modern outlook which approved knowledge has put into your hands.

The modern outlook on the Bible makes it an entrancing book, entrancingly human and entrancingly divine. It is more than ever the Book of God and Man. Perplexed ministers used to wonder how they could use the Bible in preaching, after the proved results of criticism. Why! any sane criticism—I have nothing to do with insane criticism—has only made it a book with blood in it, a book not of plaster saints, but of living, struggling, sinning and conquering men and women, a book alive with the life and problems we know, a book that enshrines God's ways with men through the generations.

In this connection may I say *preach your results and not your processes.* Assume your own position quietly and graciously, whatever it is: and preach positively, not negatively. When I say 'modern views', I don't suggest that you have either a right or a call to discuss critical questions with your people such as you discuss here in your colleges. To begin with, this would lead nowhere except to confusion with simple-hearted people. Further, it is of no religious interest, compared with the truth of your message. And lastly, we have no right to offend the religious faith of people whose belief does not rest on these results one way or the other. I would shiver to destroy some simple soul's faith, if I couldn't be sure I could put a better in its place. Here is a fine text, in the old rendering, for the young preacher, 'If I say, I will speak thus: behold I should offend against the generation of thy children.'

Perhaps I should add a word about a phrase I used a few sentences back, 'Preach your results, and not your processes!' It is never good to hear the creaking of the machinery. If you take people through your own difficulties, you will end only by making your difficulties theirs. Oddly enough, most people can state a problem or a difficulty better than they can state the solution. This is easily understood: for the problem is common, but the solution is private. I was never helped by any man's 'Way to Faith': his way is never mine. Wimmer wrote a book called *Struggle for Light*, and the only thing with which I had any community was the struggle. A minister—I can vouch for this—took his country congregation on an Easter morning through the various theories which account, on naturalistic lines, for the resurrection of Jesus. As usual, he expounded the difficulties better than his own position. In the end, an old farmer is reputed to have remarked to a fellow-member, 'I never knew before how much there was to be said against the resurrection.' It is a word of wisdom which you will find verified in later days, 'Preach your findings, and not your processes.' The best kind of engine nowadays consumes its own smoke.

5. THE SIN OF PRESUMING TOO MUCH

Under this head of message, I have still two suggestions to make, for what they are worth. You may frankly disagree with my first point: but I speak out of what experience I have had. It is this. Unless with special audiences, whom you have reason to know well, *presume that the people know little about your subject.* I am certain that we err in assuming special theological and religious knowledge in line with our own. This is the legacy, the last legacy, of a land that was once theological. It is not theological nowadays, especially among the younger generation. Never even assume a term, a technical term, although it may be a common counter in your own thinking. In all likelihood it will not be known, in your precise meaning, to five per cent of your hearers. We talk together as ministers about the Pentateuch and the Synoptic Gospels, about Eschatology or the Divine Attributes: and it is safe to say that to the average hearer these terms are only confusion worse confounded.

I think it is even wise to assume that the ordinary hearer has little grounding in either theology or religion. Though I mention it with diffidence and apology, I was greatly struck by what Principal Fairbairn suggested to me as one reason of the great success of the early Brighton ministry of Dr. R. J. Campbell. I remember him telling me, in my manse at Forres, how Dr. Campbell had started his ministry without specialised training in the theological college of his own Church, against Fairbairn's dissuasion. The Principal remarked that Dr. Campbell began to work out his own theology on independent lines each Sunday with his hearers. He took the simplest themes as the subject of his studies—the Fatherhood of God, how does Providence show itself in life? what does Jesus save us from?—themes which we unfortunately would pass off in a word or a chance paragraph. We foolishly assume, for instance, that our people know what is meant by the 'Fatherhood of God'. Do they? But Dr. Campbell worked through these big topics with his people in his own mental development, and he gained by presuming nothing. Now Fairbairn's theory about Dr. Campbell may be right or wrong: I can say nothing about it, one way or the other. But I believe Dr. Campbell's instinct was both right and fine. We lose a great power and appeal by presuming that our people know more than they do. That accounts for what we often call 'preaching over people's heads'. It is not that the man's sermon is in any sense more intellectual or searching. Real thinkers, like deep waters, are generally clear. But obscure preaching is generally due to foolish assumptions and technical terms—when it is not due to mud in the stream.

After I delivered this lecture in Glasgow, a minister in the audience kindly sent me a shrewd saying of Dr. Marcus Dods. In this matter of our 'level of treatment' for a popular audience, Dr. Dods used to say, 'Never under-estimate the intelligence of your people, but never over-estimate the use they may make of their intelligence.' This is the wisdom of experience.

6. PREACHING FOR RESULTS

My last point under the message is—preach your burden not as an interesting fact in history, but as *a dynamic for life*. Put plainly, preach for results. A sermon is not an end in itself or a work of art, but a tool. And among tools, it is a lever, to lift. You want to convince men, and lead them to Christ and the Christian way. Bring your message, therefore, down to their life, facing their problems and passions and frailties. In the best sense of the term, we seek decision. If we do not desire that, I fail to see how we can be in the line of the apostles. They at least were out for souls!

PREACHING PRESUPPOSES A PREACHER

So far I have tried to show that preaching presupposes an audience, and a message offered to them. As a last point, it presupposes a man as its vehicle. That man, the preacher, by his strength or weakness, by his broad or cribbed humanity, must give it its colour and bias. God has chosen us for His ambassadors. In one sense God has just to take us as we are. It is His glory that He can make us more than we are. If we allow the Spirit of God to work through us, even our weakness may become our strength.

I do not wish to speak, as do some lecturers on this subject, of what are called the 'personal requisites' for the ministry. At the best, that is treading on delicate ground. We all have a fear of convicting ourselves. Such questions as personal character, honesty of purpose, cleanness of life, sincerity and genuineness are best dealt with between a man's soul and God. Besides, most of our tests would be fallacious. Yet it is worth remembering, that there is nothing more likely to tell on a man's ministry in the long run than his personal character. The Sunday school teacher who most influenced my life for any good could not, as we vulgarly say, 'teach for nuts'; but the memory of his character is a shining light. It may well be that indifferent and slack men do good—God is bigger than the messenger—but in the long run it is the life that is the best ministry. 'Everything must preach in the preacher.' Samuel Butler remarks in his *Characters*, 'There is nothing so powerful to destroy any religion as the public ill example of those that profess it.'

But with your indulgence, I should like to say some things about ourselves as preachers, the man as the vehicle of the message.

1. THE COLOUR OF PERSONALITY

If preaching is a message plus a personality, the personality should have its full and natural share. What distinguishes any two preachers? Roughly speaking, if they take a common subject, most men of similar intelligence and training say largely the same things, and deal with the same aspects of truth. The main difference lies in personality, in personal touches, in personal points of view, in personal treatment, and in personal impact. All the great preachers have been strongly individualistic.

I advise you therefore to be true to your own genius, and cultivate it in its strong, natural lines. There is room for all kinds and types of preachers. The kingdom of God is richer for every variation in talent. It would be as fatal to have a monotony of brilliance as a monotony of dullness. Let your own personality, with its distinct point of view and its distinct characteristics, have its natural elbow-room. So long as you are not rudely angular or eccentric, just for the vulgar sake of being eccentric, so long as you do not violate the good laws of taste, keep to your own keel and cut your own wave! Some one has said that the message is to the preacher, as the liquid is to the bottle: 'It takes the shape of the bottle without itself suffering change.' The truth of your message will not be altered or obscured by giving it the cast and bias of your own personal outlook. Indeed, in most cases, that is gain. Let your message, therefore, be shaped and coloured by your own outlook.

2. THE GAIN AND LOSS OF MANNERISMS

We are generally told to avoid mannerisms. If by that we mean aimless tricks, conscious or unconscious, that offend the eye of the ear, no advice could be more needed or more sound. Spurgeon, in his racy lectures, shows how some little trick of manner, by endless repetition, may become so dominating and so irritating that it blots out every good point in the speaker. In the end the people cannot see the sun for its spots! Spurgeon, for instance, tells how a man may begin by nodding his head for emphasis and may end by swaying like a branch in a high wind, or rocking like a cradle.

In this particular, it is worth remembering that the eye is more easily distracted than the ear. Have you noticed this? I observed the fact, to my cost, when addressing my battalion in the open air at the Front. I found it possible to hold their attention amid distracting noises, but perilously easy to lose grip when a chance aeroplane or anything on the line of vision attracted a roving eye. If you apply this to your mannerisms, you will find that a wagging finger, swaying arms, a twitching face, gawky contortions, or a bobbing head are much more distracting—and annoying—than faults which only appeal to the ear. In one sense, the eye is less disciplined than the ear, and more subject to distraction. That is why I advise you to correct *visible* peculiarities much more carefully than vocal.

Moreover, mannerisms, like everything else, grow so quickly that we are soon the slaves of our own creation. In the end an unchecked mannerism may spoil the effectiveness of an able preacher. Be ready to take advice in this matter, and correct glaring eccentricities. Not only take advice when offered, but also ask advice from some trusted critic. Most faults may be easily corrected at the outset: in the end, they become ingrained, like habit. Personally, I should have valued advice about a vicious habit of blinking my eyes, a hundred to the minute, when excited: and though I vow each day to overcome it, I know at the end of a service, by my tired eyelids, that I have failed once more.

On the other hand, I should advise you quite frankly *not to be afraid of mannerisms unless they offend.* A mannerism means simply a 'little manner': and whether we will or no, we must possess 'manner'. After all, the style is the man. In suggesting rules for preachers, I think it would be fatal if we were turned out like bricks from a mould, however good the bricks may be in themselves. If you will forgive a personal example, I love to see how a well-known preacher in Scotland twists his face like a corkscrew and peers over his eyeglasses when he is speaking. Somehow the effect would not be the same, if he did not do it! Be decently individual then, so long as you are not self-conscious about it. Know your own gifts and limitations, the latter especially. You have distinctive qualities, each one of you: give them room and play. The only folly is to be untrue to yourself and attempt something which neither God nor man meant you to do. The more I hear of Dr. Alexander Whyte of Edinburgh, my own predecessor, the more am I amazed at his knowledge of his own gifts and sphere. He kept sedulously to his appointed measure and never attempted what he thought he could not do. An American professor told me last summer that he tried five times to tempt Dr. Whyte to lecture in America, and each time Dr. Whyte just looked at him and said, 'Man, it's not my line.' To know himself like that makes a man great.

3. THE CROWNING FOLLY OF IMITATION

The corollary of this is—*never imitate.* It is a besetting temptation when we see a man and note his power to imitate some of his typical methods. We incline to argue that if these ways and manners are the secret of his success—which of course they aren't—may they not help us? But imitation is fatal for many reasons, the chief being that we only end by imitating the other man's tricks. We are left with an empty tin that doesn't even rattle. Dr. John Kelman, and my own brother, Hugh Black, made such an individual impression on Edinburgh in their own day, that many young ministers modelled themselves on these preachers. I am told that the results were often farcical. For an average man to imitate anyone who is strongly individualistic is like fitting on a Hallowe'en mask. Sometimes—for flesh is frail—the man forgets his part, and the result is high comedy. Imitation is perilously near to parody.

4. THOU SHALT NOT STEAL

So far as you can, *acknowledge your sources.* This is only fair, and befits a gentleman. It is a nice point to enquire how far we are justified in borrowing from others. In one sense, every man deals in second-hand things, no matter how original he may be. As John Foster remarks, 'It is the privilege, the exclusive privilege, of genius to light its own fire.' Knowledge is just a vast store of truth, accumulated for us by the pioneering labours of others. Science represents the system of facts and principles which countless other workers have torn from the Sphinx. Education is a process by which we inherit truth and experience which we never could have acquired for ourselves. Our modern life, so ramified and specialised, demands that we borrow from others; and often we do not know the quarry from which our ideas were hewn. As Swift, with his sardonic tongue, puts it,

> You modern wits
> Should each man bring his claim,
> Have desperate debentures on your fame,
> And little would be left you, I'm afraid,
> If all your debts to Greece and Rome were paid.

What Frederick Robertson, of Brighton, said of himself is probably true of most men, 'I cannot copy, nor can I work out a seed of thought, developing it myself. I cannot light my own fire: but whenever I get my fire lighted from another life, I can carry the living flame as my own into other subjects, which have been illuminated in the flame.'

But while we admit that we must live generously on the labours of others, the difference between theft and honesty must never be obscured. If you borrow deliberately, admit it deliberately. You will never forfeit a good man's respect if you acknowledge indebtedness. In any case, pass the ideas you borrow from books or men through the magic alembic of your own mind. If you relate them to your own experience, and give them the tone and bias of your individual thinking, they belong in that new dress to you and nobody else. But the first and last thing is honour with oneself and God.

5. THE NOTE OF THE PROPHET

Be bold with the courage of conviction. Be bold in your message and in all good personal assurance. One of my correspondents, in answering my 'round-robin', asserted that what is lacking in the modern pulpit is the 'prophetic note'. What is this prophetic note? It does not consist, I assure you, in the type of authority criticised in my opening address, anything external, acquired from our office or standing, or from tradition and custom. But it comes only from the consciousness that we have a message of truth for the world's need laid on us as a divine charge, without which men are as wandering sheep. It was the 'burden of God' on their hearts that gave the prophets and apostles their flaming boldness. That robbed them of any fear of man, any foolish apologetic, and any laming self-distrust. They faced kings and scholars, priests and people, conscious only that all men, without distinction, needed the saving grace of God.

Can we have this? Can we recapture the prophetic note? In the first place, like the Apostles, we too can be gripped and constrained by the love of Jesus. If He is our Lord, let Him be our Lord—a Lord indeed! Further, let us see clearly that human life can only be redeemed in terms of Him. We too can be assured, equally with the disciples, that the world is lost without Him. There is no redemption in any true sense apart from Jesus. Culture fails: science fails: knowledge fails: humanity fails. In the last few years we have seen that all these vaunted 'saviours' have only heaped the world with dead: and knowledge and science have become the handmaids of refined cruelty and destruction. It is a lost world without the love and pity of Jesus: and we are lost men without His salvation. If that belief is in our hearts, like red blood, it will give us the courage of the Apostles, and will recapture for us the lost note of the prophets.

There need be no false assurance in your boldness. Certainly there should be no conceit. Some of our most courageous preachers have been the lowliest men in personal character. There is one phrase often used about successful preachers that always amazes me. People say, 'A wonderful man, and quite unspoiled by his success!' Why should he be spoiled? Is there any room for ministerial conceit and affectation? While rejoicing at being used for God's purposes, a man should only be humbled by the remembrance of his own secret imperfections and by amazed gratitude that God can use him for His high ends.

Be bold! Be not too bold!

3 The Smith at his Forge

Work is my sore burden, but it is also my great resource. I eat my heart out when I am not up to my neck in work: there you have the secret of the life I lead.

SAINTE-BEUVE, writing to a friend

SOURCES OF POWER

I. PRELIMINARIES

As the years go by—more so in later years, the true testing time—your success as a minister may depend on one or two things.

(*a*) *Your idea of the ministry*, your notion of what your business is, and what you are out for. This is the ultimate secret of success, now, and especially twenty years hence. A minister's ideal of preaching is the real power-room of his preaching. What are we trying to do Sunday by Sunday? What is at the back of all our effort? In the last resort, a man can only expect to hit what he aims at, unless he believes that one can do good by flukes. Inadequate views—especially when the glamour has worn off—manufacture most of life's inadequate ministries. I do not know anything just so tragic as a man who is doomed to preach what is not real to himself, or who discharges his office because it *is* an office. But if we have a true idea of our function as preachers—to commend the love of God, and win men and women for Him and the good life in Jesus—that of itself will sort everything else into its true place and importance. Most of all, it will make us faithful in our preparation: it will lead us to train and harness every good gift in its service: it will impart a clear genuineness to our speech. I do not want to dogmatise to you, but I feel inclined to say that it would be a gain to the Church and to yourselves if you gave up the ministry rather than enter it with blurred views about Jesus and the needs of the human soul. Our work is a *vocation*, not a job. We are in God's business: we handle His affairs: and we traffic for souls. You will soon find that even careless men will forgive the absence of anything in a minister except conviction and fine sincerity. I have met men who labelled me with all manner of names—'bigot', 'unpractical', 'bull-headed', and what not—but I have never yet met a man who in his secret soul did not respect a minister for his Christian convictions, and did not despise him for their absence.

(*b*) *Your stored resources of knowledge and experience*, all the burden of truth and wisdom you have acquired, knowledge plus experience in happy combination. A minister is continually giving out week by week, even if it be only in 'penny packets', and there must be some method of refilling the coffer. Real joy in preaching depends on our having more ideas and suggestions for preaching than we can ever use: and this fine joy, akin to elation, only comes when our minds, and notebooks, are crammed full. The best preaching is always *the natural overflow* of a ripe mind and the expression of a growing experience. A good sermon is never worked up but worked out.

You have to see, therefore, that your store is replenished as quickly as it is used, that your mind retains interest and movement, and that your experience is maturing like wheat in the ear. Otherwise, there may be a new rendering of the ancient and pitiful tragedy of Mother Hubbard. That moving drama of the absent bone and the suffering dog is one of the gems of literature for the ministry. Instead of the trite tags with which a species of minister adorns his mantelshelf, telling all and sundry to 'do it now', just write on a slip of paper this motto, 'Remember Mother Hubbard!' As Milton complains in *Lycidas*, 'The hungry sheep look up and are not fed.'

Your richness for your future ministry will depend in strict proportion on the richness of your own mind and soul. Often in ministering to others, we forget the primary duty of ministering to ourselves. Growing people in the pew are only helped by a growing mind in the pulpit. Cultivate above all things your own devotional and spiritual life, so that your vision becomes clearer and your insight keener each day. This is the only way in which we can be sure of having 'the best wine' at the end, a ministry undimmed and undwindling. I remember asking Dr. Campbell Morgan if he prepared his prayers before going into the pulpit, and he answered somewhat cryptically, 'I try to prepare myself.' We need the type of preparation round which necessarily these lectures must gather: but above and before everything else, we need an increasing preparation of ourselves, a preparation of heart and head alike. I do not see how one can fill anything from an empty cask.

For mental richness, the moral of this lies in one thing, *application*, which is a minor form of genius, sometimes more fruitful than genius. There are few things denied to passion and labour combined. The Duke of Wellington used to say that British soldiers were not braver than French soldiers, but were only braver five minutes longer! But the secret of all success lies there.

(*c*) Progress will depend on *trained quickness and readiness of thought and expression.* At first, as I remember to my cost, the task of writing two sermons a week, to say nothing of a Prayer Meeting and a Bible Class, with a few extras thrown in as ballast, produced a kind of mental paralysis. But a man of ordinary gifts and resources quickly discovers that faithfulness brings its own proportionate reward in increasing aptitude and readiness of mind. As a result, what was once a bogey becomes a pleasure, the artist's pleasure in creative work, than which I question if there is a finer in the world. It is one of the subtle joys of the ministry to discover that as you use your weapon, it sharpens itself: and in time, it fits the shape of your hand. Practice alone brings this readiness, and makes us quick workers. And if I may confess it, it is only this acquired readiness that makes a ministry in a large congregation possible or manageable. Only, I beg you, never play or presume on that growing readiness. An increasing facility is something worth praying and labouring for: but there is such a thing as a 'fatal facility'. For most men, ease of speech is only a gilded curse. I know of more speakers who fail by their fatal fluency of thought and expression than by any self-distrust or hesitancy. 'Keep back thy servant, also, from presumptuous sins.'

(*d*) Progress will depend also on developing *our gift of teaching* and power of handling and applying truth. Fortunately, this can be cultivated: I even believe it can be acquired, where absent. Any person who can learn can surely examine his own methods of learning. Some self-knowledge is the real secret of teaching. To put yourself, mentally and spiritually, in the other man's place, and from that, begin to teach yourself—I am sure that is the way to teach others. The man who cannot teach has always a suspicion of the fool about him: for this proves that he does not understand the mental processes by which he himself learns.

(*e*) Progress and success will depend on *some faculty for arrangement and method* in your work. Your order may not be another man's—to him it may be sheer disorder—but I think you must have method and proportion of some kind. I know that my own methods, my desk for instance, would scare many a prim precisian; but, nevertheless, I have the order that seems to suit me. Don't be hectored into believing that you ought to adopt those artificial docketing methods that suit a business man or a railway-ticket office—schedules, systems, fancy drawers with tickets on wires. Personally, that type of thing would wring me as dry as a sucked orange. But nevertheless, have the distinct methods that suit yourself and your work, and then honour them. You can have any methods you like, so long as you have methods.

Under this, may I insert a note about method in congregational work, though that is hardly in place here. But it may prove helpful. I have had experience of two congregations with a roll of about 1,500 to 1,600 members. Looking at that, with other varied duties—among them, Warrack and Sprunt lectures and such little oddments—it seems a little stupendous and paralysing. But reduce it for a moment to order and method. Roughly, it means, in the one church, 800 visits, and in the second, owing to more individual calls and fewer families, near 1,000 visits. Take the bigger figure, and resolve simply to get round in two or three years. If you take two years, that means 500 visits per year. Now if you only do twenty visits per week—which means roughly ten to twelve hours—and if you only visit twenty-five weeks out of the fifty-two, you have your five hundred visits. I mention this simply because I have done it. Do not look at the big task as a stark staring whole, or you will get stage-fright and mental impotence. Look at each day with its prescribed job by itself. One step at a time is good walking.

(*f*) Once more, in preliminary. I beg you not to wait for 'inspiration' as one waits for a glint of sunshine on a dull day. I believe that you can often *command* inspiration. If honest work will not command it, what will? We are sometimes too finical about our work, especially its form. I have known men who ought to have written a big book, work which the Church had a right to expect from them, but they waited for the inspiration to make the thing perfect. And they, and we, are waiting still. Get to business faithfully, and that effort of itself, with God's Spirit, will bring the afflatus. Someone spoke to Dr. Johnson of 'happy moments' for composition. 'Nay,' said Johnson, 'a man may write at any time, if he will set himself doggedly to it.'

I admit of course that there *are* happy moments, angel-visits; and when they come, they are a golden rain! (The man who dreams them away in an arm-chair beggars his own ministry.) But the point is—are they worth waiting for in a week that has only seven days? And further, will they come if they are waited for! I prophesy that if we sit down to wait for their coming, they will visit us less and less, dwindling away like the Sibylline Books of Roman mythology. I am sure that honest work is the one great secret—even of inspiration. In any case, it keeps the machinery well oiled and in good order, ready for 'the big push' when it comes. Otherwise, like a motor-car on a frosty day, the spark may find the engine cold, and cranking will be time-wasting labour! The best way to use inspiration when it comes is to have the machine well warmed beforehand.

These may be called counsels of perfection. But would any other kind of counsel be worthy of you or the subject? Remember the old tag, 'Little things make perfection, but perfection is not a little thing.'

INDIRECT PREPARATION

There are two great types of preparation for our work—on the one hand *direct preparation*, which lies strictly within the compass of each week, and on the other hand, *indirect preparation*, which lies spread out over the years, and whose value consists in what these years have meant for us in mental and spiritual richness.

I choose to speak first about our indirect preparation for our ministry, because in the long run this is either more telling or more disastrous than immediate preparation week by week. I shall confine myself to four points, which I think mean much for our future effectiveness.

I. THE GOSPEL OF THE TREADMILL

The gospel of the treadmill, in your study, with your jacket off, sheer grim work among your books. A man's future does not come to him out of to-morrow but out of yesterday. Stephen Leacock—humorist, professor, and gardening enthusiast—remarked that the only way to garden successfully is to begin the year before last. And the only way to preach well is to begin ten years ago. Your future lies in germ in the preparation of your early days. In frank moments, most ministers could testify that they personally are less of a power to-day because of the work they scamped in their college hours. Life holds a delicate scale of subtle punishment: and I would save you from vain regrets.

Your professors will readily admit that your greatest gain here is not the accumulation of the facts and theories they have taught you, but rather a habit of study, a disciplined mind, the student outlook and a point of view. If you have that student mind, your future is largely secure, so far as you can command it.

Your danger, after you leave college, will lie in the fact that you will be your own master, working at your own pressure and at your own times, and answerable only to your own conscience. Your faithfulness will depend on the kind of conscience you have. Make up for the loss of prescribed tasks—by prescribing tasks for yourselves. It is a pity—and the source of much failure—that so many of us cease to be students after we leave the eagle eye of our professors. I assure you, as students, that a big ministry is more often the fruit of hard work than the fruit of genius. And in this matter of a needed spur for work, if you miss the gimlet eye of the professor, you can remember that other eye that never sleeps.

2. COURSES OF READING

I do not know that I have anything helpful to say about reading. I should advise you, however, to follow Martin Luther's advice, given in his *Table Talk*, to have some 'sure and certain books' which you know as well as you know your best friend, books which in Bacon's phrase are 'to be chewed and digested'. And secondly, I would say, as a complementary truth, that if you have any special study of your own—and I think you should have, something you resolve to know as well as anybody can know it—the rest of your reading will only gain by being as desultory and vagrant and browsing as possible. Still, there are certain lines about which a minister in these days ought to have some competent knowledge. Otherwise he will be tested and found wanting. Although you will soon be beyond the prying examination of professors, you will be examined before another fairly critical tribunal, the men and women in your congregation who are sure to know more about some subjects than you do, even if it is only the farm labourer who knows more about crops and soils.

May I make the following suggestions?

(*a*) I think you should be conversant with the progress of present-day science, our modern Alice-in-Wonderland. Men are discovering that the world is a big thing, and a big world means a big God. If we are to honour and worship Him worthily, we must know His works. On all grounds, for their own sake and for the truth they teach, ministers should know and respect the discoveries of the human mind. Religion cannot be buttressed by obscurantism but only by truth. Even a periodical like *Nature* will keep you up in a working knowledge of what is being done and discovered month by month. (*New Scientist* is excellent. Ed.)

(*b*) You should know modern psychology, even in its run-away and 'Freudian' views. You should know these views even if you don't profess them. This type of reading is wholly cognate to your work, a knowledge of men and motives. In any study of character and conduct, some intimate knowledge of psychology is clearly essential.

(*c*) Beyond doubt, any 'live' ministry, by personal experience and by study, must be acquainted with social needs and social experiments. It is our duty to be interested in a clean State, pure civic conditions, and good living. We know to our cost what part environment plays in the formation of character and ideals. While we believe that character can be formed gloriously in any environment, we know that there are prevalent conditions of life that make goodness a hard, if not impossible thing. Flowers grow best in a good seed-bed. If we desire the one, we should attend to the other.

(*d*) I recommend a good working knowledge of politics and institutions. (By the way, the more you keep politics out of your pulpit, the better, remembering, however, that we claim the right to speak on moral issues that affect the kingdom of God.) But if you are not interested in politics, you ought at least to be acquainted with some general political theory. Apart from other considerations, history with biography is the most fruitful source of moving illustration.

3. HOURS FOR WORK

As a general rule in regard to work, claim your morning hours. Dr. Denney used to tell his students that we should distrust all work done by 'artificial light'. That, of course, is quite debatable. Even if it be admitted that one writes with too much colour and stress by gaslight, still it is better 'to compose with fury and correct with phlegm, than to compose with phlegm and correct with fury'. The creative faculty is often strongest at night, perhaps dangerously imaginative. On the other hand, the morning hours may find us too coldly critical and sluggish. But naturally, if a man is healthy and living normally, he is freshest in the morning. Reserve these golden hours jealously for yourselves, not for casual discursive reading but for something purposeful. You need not be boorish or rude, but nevertheless I advise you to frighten callers away tactfully in the morning! Do you remember the tragedy of the 'Man from Porlock'?

I nearly passed on without explaining that allusion. In case I forget to say it later on, let me say it now—never deal in allusions in your sermon, literary or otherwise. They appear smart and give a flavour of culture and learning, though the flavour may be as dubious as the culture. They please that strain of foolish vanity that lies deep in the best of us, and they tickle a few stray hearers who think themselves literary. But you are preaching to simple souls whom you have no right to puzzle with literary gymnastics.

In case you forget the tragedy of the 'Man from Porlock', let me explain. Coleridge was reading *Purchas's Pilgrimes* when he fell asleep with this sentence haunting his mind, 'Here the Khan Kubla commanded a palace to be built, and a stately garden thereunto.' In the morning he started to write the poem that had been born in his mind during sleep. But a man from Porlock—nameless, thank Heaven!—called to see Coleridge about some trumpery business. Instead of sending the man from Porlock—back at least to Porlock—Coleridge went out and discussed with him some trivial things, no doubt that perennial topic the state of the weather: and when he came back, the poem was lost beyond recall. Tell that story gently and tactfully to your congregation some day!

Anthony Trollope's recipe for literary work is worth giving you. His advice is to put a piece of soft cobbler's wax on your study chair, and then sit on it. That provides what we call 'security of tenure'.

I shall finish this point with two short quotations. The first is from Sir Joshua Reynolds' *Discourses*. 'If you have great talents, industry will improve them; if you have but moderate talents, industry will supply their deficiency. Nothing is denied to well-directed labour; nothing is to be obtained without it.'

The second is from O. Wendell Holmes' *Elsie Venner*. 'Remember that a young man, using large endowments wisely and fortunately, may put himself on a level with the highest in the land in ten years of spirited and unflagging work.' Believe that; but be sure you make it 'spirited and unflagging work'.

In the ministry, of all places, God has no use for a lazy man. By the way, a man's 'laziness' often consists not in idleness but in doing very busily what he should be doing at some more appropriate time. There is an Eastern proverb which says, 'You can only take out of a pot what you put into it.' Unless you are a juggler, you can only take rabbit-pie out, if you have put some raw material in. You can only take out of your sermons what you have put into them in hard work, passion and spiritual vision.

'Tis God gives skill,
But not without men's hands: He could not make
Antonio Stradivari's violins
Without Antonio. Get thee to thy easel!

Work of this kind is good and will bring you a mature reward. But need I say to the average healthy student that all work and no play makes Jack a dull boy? I commend to you a decent hobby, and ask you to ride it. 'Ride it,' I said, lest you be ridden! I think you should have interests entirely beyond your work, big enough, occasionally, to make you forget your work. I do not care what these interests are, so long as they are real interests. Personally, did I not know that it is an inborn gift like poetry, I should commend to you *a love of roses*.

In finishing this point, I shall offer you an important piece of advice, if you will promise not to smile at it—when you have done your best and put grit into your work, the best preparation for the Sunday is a good sleep on Saturday night! It stands to reason that if you bring a tired body and a fagged mind to your services, you can't give of your best. Any flash you may have is only hectic. Look sharply after your health and fitness.

4. THE NOTING EYE

Next to work and reading, I place *common observation* of men and things. 'Books are good enough in their own way,' says R. L. Stevenson, 'but they are a mighty bloodless substitute for life.' Herbert Spencer used to say, with dry humour, that if he had read as much as other men, he would know as little as they did! A man can lose himself in other people's thoughts. Indeed, I have known men who picked up a book just to escape thinking.

You are dealing with people, and you must know people. You must know their daily life, their struggles and temptations, our little shameful meannesses and our wonderful heroisms, the piece of work we call 'man'. Self-knowledge is good, but it is not enough: for there is always the chance that you yourself may be unique, if not odd! Get to know others, their ways of thinking, their points of view, the emotions that touch them, and most of all, their frailties and glories.

To begin with, your best illustrations will come from your daily observation of men and things. Some ministers, I notice, possess books of illustrations neatly indexed under headings. If you have a 'noting eye', you will find a much better and more living book in the first village and congregation where you are settled. And further, if you observe with sympathy the lives of men and women, you will learn one secret of power and interest in preaching—to discuss some question with an individual in your mind. I do not mean 'preaching at' individuals. That, to say the least of it, is 'below the belt'. But we should often preach with some known case beneath our eyes, provided we are discreet enough to avoid the insolence of a pointing finger. You can have this assurance, so like is humanity, that if you help one, you will help hundreds.

5. SERMONS IN STONES

Cultivate the 'Homiletic Mind'. This is a hideous phrase, but you know what I mean. I was chatting with a shoemaker the other day, and he made this remark: 'When I meet people, the first thing I look at is their shoes.' That is a cobbler's 'homiletic mind'. A poet comes to regard everything he sees and feels as so much poetic material, and quite rightly. My family says—with bias, of course—that I ruin our holiday each year by collecting from every odd whinbush the material for a children's sermon. Now, I do not say that you should go through life prosing and sermonising. We all detest the professional moraliser who, besides being a bore, only spoils God's green world for himself and others. But I do say with the Duke in *As You Like It*, that you can find sermons in stones and good in everything. A wise minister may bring strange grist to his mill from his own experience. There is usually something delightfully unhackneyed in such material, for it comes to the hearer as fresh as a breath from the hills or as a sprig of heather. Only take one warning! The Session-clerk of an Edinburgh church used to say that the congregation made it a practice to send their minister to the Holy Land after twenty-five years' ministry, and then they regretted it for the next twenty-five! 'When I was in the Holy Land.' 'I once saw in Jerusalem.' 'I remember in Jericho.' You can imagine how stale and wearisome it becomes!

6. WITH PEN IN HAND

I have left this to the last, because it is the most important. *Know your Bible as a book, even as literature, apart from criticism and exegesis.* It is here that the finest indirect preparation for the pulpit appears. As you read—I don't mean 'reading for texts', which is a ghastly travesty of the devotional reading of the Bible—as you read, if anything strikes you, jot it down. I keep a book for this purpose. I jot down whatever text subject or passage appeals to me; and I jot down at once the thought or train of thought it has suggested to my mind. It is not enough to jot down the text without the impression, for if you do, you will soon find that your impression is very fugitive. I have jotted down many texts, and wondered afterwards why in all the world I had recorded them at all. Take a page or half a page of your book, and detail what has impressed you at the moment. It may prove barren afterwards, but you never can tell! The gain in such a practice is immense. First of all, a text thus obtained is likely to be one you can use with freshness and interest. For it is the text that finds and grips you, which is most likely to find and grip your hearers. Your strongest sermons will be on the subjects which have sprung out from the passage and hit you between the eyes. They claim you and command attention. Further, this saves you from the week-end tragedy of hunting for subjects, a dreary and soul-scarifying performance. And still further, this offers you a subject on which you already have a line, like a fish on a hook. To change the metaphor, you have meat there, partly digested.

DIRECT PREPARATION

With this said, asking you to forgive omissions, I should like to say something about the direct preparation of your sermon, once you have your text subject or passage selected.

1. THOROUGH PREPARATION

At the beginning of your ministry at least, this direct preparation cannot be too minute or thorough. It is reported that Professor Mackintosh of Edinburgh once said that after a man had been some years in the ministry, he ought to find his subject and finish his sermon within eight working hours. I do not know whether Professor Mackintosh really said that: in any case, I consider it a wise saying. But that facility, like wisdom, 'lingers'. At the beginning, however, for your own future good, you cannot put too much grind into your preparation. Hard toil for one sermon makes every succeeding one easier.

A noted evangelist once came to address us at Glasgow College. As a piece of solemn and considered advice, he recommended us sometimes to go into the pulpit, find our text on the spur of the moment, and preach, trusting in inspiration for our message. Professor Denney was in the chair. I shall never forget that white face and that wagging finger as he turned to the speaker and said with his incisive passion, 'We are here in this College, set aside by the Church, to tell these men that there is no preparation too sacred or solemn for the ministry of Jesus Christ, and you come now and try to undo our work with these students. I think, Sir, you confuse inspiration with desperation!' And I might add on my own, 'with perspiration'!

2. TEXT AND CONTEXT

When you have chosen your text or passage, get to know its exact rendering and translation, and its place in its own context. Wise George Herbert, hard to beat by any modern adviser, writes in his old-fashioned way: 'The parson's method in handling of a text consists of two parts: First a plain and evident declaration of the meaning of the text: and secondly, some choice observations drawn out of the whole text, as it lies entire, and unbroken in the Scripture itself. This he thinks natural, and sweet and grave.' We have no right to pick up a text as if it were a stray pebble. We are not going to import a meaning into it, but take a definite and precise meaning out of it. It is absolutely necessary for us to make sure of our foundations before we start to build. In his essay on *Building*, Francis Bacon remarks: 'He that builds a fair house upon an ill seat committeth himself to prison.' I have no use for a lovely sermon that is built on a wrong exegesis. The man who does that is trifling with three things that ought to be sacred for anyone of intellectual honesty—he trifles with truth, his people, and the message of the Bible. Sometimes you will find that a true rendering—as often, for instance, in the Book of Proverbs—spoils the accepted sense of the Authorised Version. But if you are faithful to the true rendering, it is likely to give you something even more massive. For example, I once heard a sermon on the text, 'Where there is no vision the people perish.' The preacher took his text at its face value, using the word 'vision' wrongly, and the word 'perish' wrongly. It is not true, historically, that where there is no vision the people perish. They do *not* perish—they keep living on! But if you examine a decent commentary, you will discover that the word rendered 'perish' really means 'break-up' or 'go to pieces', like a doll that has been out in the rain overnight and has become 'undone'. The pieces are all there, but they have lost cohesion. Now, there is a powerful and searching sermon in the real translation, that where there is no prophet's word, or guidance, or law of God, people break up or go to pieces, come to moral smash. That is a greater tragedy than to be wiped out. Oblivion is often an oblique mercy.

Another instance: 2 Corinthians 5:17 says, 'If any man be in Christ, a new creation.' Textually, you may supply either 'he is' or 'there is'. With the first you have the great view of man made a new creature in Jesus, and the wonder and glory of it. With the other, you have the complementary truth that a man in Jesus Christ soon discovers that the world he lives in is new and dazzling for him. He sees everything differently—life, his fellowmen, sin, death and the future. He is changed and the world is changed.

3. LAST THINGS FIRST

Having your text and subject, and knowing their implication, you have now to define and delimit your message. If I may speak personally—I suppose that is what you want—the first thing I generally get is my 'conclusion', *what I want to be at.* A wise traveller, in considering his journey, looks first to the goal. I feel somehow that everything else has got to lead up and contribute to that. In this case, the last should be first.

Your message in its compass may divide itself into points, complementary or contrasting. If it does, do not be ashamed to announce your divisions. There are some hypersensitive ministers who think it artistic to conceal divisions, as if they were something indecent, or at least a little indelicate. Paley remarks that 'a discourse which rejects these aids to perspicuity may turn out a bewildered rhapsody, without aim or effect, order or conclusion'. Sometimes, as with a single-topic sermon, you may not need divisions. But where they are naturally there, for clearness to yourself and others, announce them frankly. They are there, and must be there, all the time, as clear division marks or steps of transition. Whether you announce them or no, plan them in your own mind in order of sequence and development. If there is any coherence in your own thinking, your divisions will never be artificial. Beware of what George Herbert calls 'crumbling a text up into small parts'.

I am quite sure that the finest thing in a sermon is when it conveys the idea of progress or distinct movement, a march, where the one idea follows from the other as you would draw out a telescope. There is nothing that engages and charms an intelligent audience like progress. If it isn't there, all the brilliant things you can say, unrelated, will not redeem the sermon from the taint of being hotchpotch. A sermon is like a journey: you want to arrive somewhere. When you do arrive, finish strongly, with the natural climax or application of your truth. Never finish with anything that has been already presupposed in your previous remarks. In any kind of speaking, that is lame: and it dissipates the natural effect of your message. Besides, it is not a climax, but an anticlimax.

4. THE SPADE AND THE RAKE

But I am going ahead of myself. First of all, jot down, without any pretension of order or arrangement, everything you can say or think helpfully on your subject. It does not matter whether it proves to be ultimately relevant or no: if it comes into your mind in thinking of your subject, jot it down. If it seems a cognate thought or illustration, jot it down. If I were to apply a garden simile, I should advise two processes: (*a*) *Use your spade*, to 'dig' your subject, to turn it well over and loosen it out, to get straight down into its depth and meaning. And here, as in gardening, 'double-trenching' always pays, for it loosens the bottom layer! And (*b*), *use your rake*, to gather into a heap about you every good thing that will enrich your matter and treatment. At first, you cannot gather in too much: never mind at the moment whether it is useful or no. The point is—use your rake!

I have a way of my own in this matter which I mention for what it is worth. When I have my text or subject, I put a series of questions to it and try to make it answer them. I box its ears something like this: 'What do you mean? What did you mean for that man in his own day? Why was he led to say this? Can you stand on your own legs, or are you only a dwarfed half-truth? Are you true always? Do you mean the same for me to-day? What would it imply for me if I accepted what you teach? What principles or duties do you involve for me? Is there anything to be said on the other side? What must I do to make your message real and true in my own life? How can I illustrate modernly what you teach for myself and others? How can I best drive you home at the spear-point?' I do not know if that device seems silly to you: but I find it profitable to make my subject answer a string of questions like that. If your net is big enough and the mesh fine enough, there is not much that should manage to slip through.

When you have exhausted your subject—or yourself—there before you, scattered and higgledy-piggledy, is your material, all you can think or say usefully on the subject, all that will influence thought, touch the conscience, and move the will. If this has been done early in the week, and you have time on your side, I should rise and leave it. Go out of doors and do some visiting. A change of work is a rest: and time clarifies the mind.

5. THE ART OF THE BLUE PENCIL

The next process is what I call the *Riddle*, to sift and sort things out. (Forgive these garden similes!) The best riddle, of course, is the plan or progress, the natural linking or development of the idea in the raw material itself. There should be some logical arrangement or order: otherwise it is not thinking, as we understand thinking. Apply your own plan in such a way that it 'shakes out' irrelevant things, as a dog shakes water from its coat.

Once you have that development, use your blue pencil. *The art of the blue pencil* is a priceless gift in preaching. Cut out everything that is irrelevant, or needless, or redundant, or distracting. More sermons are ruined by 'going off at a tangent' than by anything else. Too much material may be worse than too little. Sometimes the people cannot see the wood for the trees. I should like to say quite definitely that preachers and speakers are mainly distinguished by their use of the art of omission. It is a glorious art. It explains the secret of success or failure, more than any other single thing in the 'craft' of preaching. In speaking of Leigh Hunt's garrulous essays, Edmund Gosse remarks that he was 'unacquainted with the virtues of the jelly-bag'. The jelly-bag is excellent both for kitchen and study—provided we value a clear product!

A fine speaker makes his point with ease and natural fullness, and adds nothing more. He denies himself interesting side-issues, which however would only obscure the main subject for the average hearer. He strains out unnecessary phrases, and especially those fat purple adjectives. He deletes an otherwise fine thought that is not quite consonant with the main idea. He forbids himself hedging remarks, such as 'On the other hand', or 'This may be considered'. It can be considered another time. God sparing you, you are going to preach in that church a few Sundays more.

6. STRAIGHT LINES OR TANGENTS

In this connection may I add—do not be afraid of exaggeration. Isolation of any kind is exaggeration: and when you isolate a text or subject from the whole coherent body of truth, you exaggerate it in the very process. State your main truth, in the distinct and even limited aspect you have chosen, and trust to the correcting influence of your whole ministry. There is nothing so futile as aiming at a foolish completeness. In the old days, ministers could crush all theology into one sermon. But then, they only preached one sermon, though they took different texts! Their texts were pretexts. But we preach, or should preach, textually: and texts or passages only contain aspects of truth. Unless it is patent that something complementary should be said, let your text or passage do its own definite and limited work, and avoid refinements, additions and hedging comments. Later on, you will notice that most fine speakers excel in the art of omission, what Gosse calls the 'jelly-bag', an art that applies to irrelevant words and phrases as well as irrelevant and hedging ideas. Get into your subject, and keep strictly to your subject.

I admit, of course, that some minds are charmingly digressive. They do not think in a straight line but in little odd tangents like a spray of leaves. When that is done well—and it needs to be done well—it may be a sheer delight. It is this fine quality of irresponsibility—as if one should say, 'Now that reminds me'—that gives a good essayist his charm. He wanders from one thing to another as waywardly as a cow eats grass. But while this may be occasionally interesting and arresting in the hands of a genius, it is like good pastry compared with good bread. You want the plain wholesome stuff for ordinary diet.

7. EXIT THE INTRODUCTION

In the application of this gift of omission, I should include the elaborate and detailed introduction. Often there is not the slightest call for this introduction at all. Where there is a need, sketch your preamble quickly, vividly, graphically, pictorially if possible. Let the audience see the situation in a few nervous phrases, like the strokes of an artist's brush. Once this is done, get ahead into your subject. I speak on this point because, with a view to these lectures and for my own sins I have gone back and examined some of my early sermons. I never saw such lop-sided creations in my life. If one could reverse phrases and call the introduction the tail, then the tail wagged the dog. Fine writing in these introductions! I could not do it now to save my life! But the very fineness of the writing only showed up the poorness of what followed. In one sermon of eight pages, I had three pages of introduction. Now, to say the least, that is want of balance: and, in any case, it is poor art.

8. METHODS OF TREATMENT

Sometimes I have found it useful, besides giving variety, to state the problem first, if I am dealing with a problem. I try to show how the question is a living and pressing thing, and how it affects the puzzled man to-day. Having done so, I turn and say something like this, 'Now, that is a real modern problem with which you men and women are closely concerned. May I ask you to notice how that problem arose in the situation before us, and how the writer or speaker dealt with it?' When you do something like that, by way of variety of course, the attention of the audience is engaged to see how their own difficulties are dealt with in the incident you have chosen. They listen to the passage and your exposition with a new light and interest, for they look at it with their own problem before them. In other words, they have a ruling idea in their mind, with which they measure the passage.

I mention this only as an example of a legitimate use of design in presenting your material. Any art is good, if it isn't merely an artifice. In the same way, I have occasionally employed the Italian method of introduction—at least it was given me by a Waldensian student as being a typical style of Waldensian sermon. The minister stands up, announces his text, and says, 'I desire in my address to establish the following positions: (1) So-and-so, (2) So-and-so, and (3) So-and-so.' Then he proceeds with his sermon and subject.

I refer to this for good variety. As you can see, it has obvious dangers. It gives your whole situation away. You lay your cards on the table. If your cards are not very good, you are done before you begin. But if your points are strong and interesting, you may engage the people's attention in wondering how you deduce your conclusions from your premises. But that will be mainly an intellectual interest, and you may lose the finest interest of all, *surprise*. I believe in legitimate arrest. It is fatal to let your people know the inside of your mind, so that they could almost make a wager how you are going to treat your subject. If a minister has only one stereotyped method, a congregation hearing him Sunday after Sunday soon gets to know his official way of thinking, and especially his official way of *dividing* his thinking. Therefore, cultivate variety in handling your material. Variety is the spice of 'continuous' preaching.

So important is *variety* that you will forgive me emphasising it in a paragraph of its own. I advise you to cultivate variety in your pulpit work in every good way that suggests itself. Most people tire of any one diet of food, no matter how excellent and rich the diet is—indeed, the richer it is, the quicker they tire of it! A thoughtful jail-bird once told me that the biggest bit of Hell in prison life is not prison conditions or prison isolation, but prison sameness, the simple fact that *there is no change*. I believe it is fatal if people once think that they know *how we think*! Defy them to do it by changing your method and procedure. Go forwards one day, and backwards the next. Go from the centre to the circumference, and then from the circumference to the centre. Preach a bit of logic, stiff as steel, one Sunday, and a sheer bit of poetry (if it is in you) the next. Preach occasionally with a paint-brush, especially when you are dealing with portraits. Give the people a string of facts one week, and a dream or a fantasy the following. If we cling to one type, no matter how good, it will prove in the end a stick for our own backs. And in the same way, vary your methods and style, so long as you are not artificial or strained. If you will not misunderstand me, I think it is a good thing to come up to church some Sunday, saying to yourself, 'Now I defy anybody in this church to guess how I am going to treat this subject.' I do not want you to be mental acrobats: but at least do not be the slaves of your own self-imposed methods. There is no prisoner just so pathetic as the man who is his own prisoner!

I have a jotting in my Common-Place Book from Ward Beecher, a real prince of speakers: and from our point of view, his advice is as wise a sentence as he ever wrote. 'When you have finished your sermon, not a man of your congregation should be unable to tell you, distinctly, what you have done: but when you begin your sermon, no man in the congregation ought to be able to tell you what you are going to do.'

9. FINISH BEFORE YOU BEGIN

Regarding your material, now gathered, arranged and digested, I have one general counsel to offer. If you write—I shall speak of that in a later lecture—if you write, do not put pen to paper until you could stand up and talk it all out point by point to a friend. You cannot expect to write clearly and exactly until your thinking is definite and orderly. Stand up and say to your imaginary friend, 'I am going to preach on this subject. I shall begin with this aspect showing what it means and implies, as thus and thus. I shall pass then to this, which I think follows naturally. That will lead me to this further fuller development. Then I shall pass naturally to this other aspect. And finally I shall bring the hammer down on that and that. And then I finish.' Some people tell me that writing helps them to think, as if the act of composition aided their mental processes. Personally, I like to do my thinking before I write: I want to know *what* I am going to write.

I am afraid I cannot understand a minister—I have one in my

mind—who described to me his method of writing in the following terms. 'I sit down and start my sermon. Then I stop and bite my pen. Then another point comes, and I get that down. Another bite to my pen! And often I am led in my writing from one thing to another, until I finish quite differently from what I planned.' Somehow I cannot conceive of a man 'finishing up' differently from what he planned, because the conclusion, *what he wants to be at*, is the first thing he should have. This text or passage—take any one—teaches this quite definite truth or forces us to this or that definite decision. That is what we want to drive home: everything else should contribute to that. Otherwise, unless your plan itself was wrong, you began with the wrong conclusion. I should describe that minister's sermon as 'extempore writing', which is even a shade worse than extempore speaking.

Mr. Stacey Aumonier, in discussing the art of the short story—himself a master of the craft—remarks, 'This is the point which cannot be stressed too much—that a short story must be finished before it is begun. In other words, you must think it all out clearly and in detail, before you begin to write.' This advice applies even more pertinently to a sermon. It should be finished, in your own mind, point by point, and link by link, before it is begun. And I repeat, the first thing you should get is your conclusion.

10. JOINING THE LINKS

When you come to composition, one thing to study is what we call 'juncturæ', your joinings or transitions between point and point. It is true, as someone has said, that 'stones well cut need little cement'. They lie neatly together, with no yawning ungainly gaps. Sometimes of course you will deal in contrasts. But curiously enough, contrasts always agree together. They are so clean-cut that the transition is easy and natural. The difficulty and awkwardness often arise from allied points that develop out of each other in telescope fashion. I think the one thing hearers never follow easily is a 'leap' or 'jump' in one's thinking. In fact, this leap is very often the reason why some speakers are charged with obscurity. Chesterton shows in his refreshing estimate of Browning that the poet is never 'obscure'. Any imagined obscurity is due to the fact that he makes unexpected leaps, for which he has not sufficiently prepared his readers. His thought is orderly and logical enough, but he has suppressed or overlooked some links in the chain. Hence the obscurity! Now your purpose is to be 'understood of the people'. Therefore take all legitimate precautions to avoid obscurities of manner or subject. And meanwhile be content—it is a fine humbling discipline for your mind—be content to crawl and go surely, lest you only dazzle some simple soul. You are not there to dazzle but give light. And you are not there to be clever!

II. THE ART OF FINISHING

With the material sketched and ordered and linked, you come to the most important thing of all, *how to sit down.* Oliver Wendell Holmes, in his quaint and quizzical way, describes visitors in a drawing-room. 'Don't you know how hard it is for some people to get out of a room after their visit is really over? They want to be off, and you want them to be off, but they don't know how to manage it. One would think they had been built in your parlour or study, and were waiting to be launched.' This is a happy description of many a speaker, especially an extempore or at least unprepared speaker. He wants to finish—you can see it in his glassy eye!—and you want him to finish. But he cannot secure a decent or effective exit: so he takes another aimless amble round the room! There is a story told of a north-country preacher in Scotland who was rather noted for his difficulty in coming to an end. A parishioner who had not been to church, as he passed the door, saw a worshipper slipping out. He asked the escaping culprit if the minister were done? 'Aye,' said the man vindictively, 'he's done, but he winna stop.'

It is a pity if our finish should finish us, and waste an otherwise good general impression. It is worth remembering that the final impression of a speech or a sermon is the one that lasts longest and clearest. A strong finish rings in our ears like the chimes of a bell. May I venture to say a few words on this art of finishing?

In one sense, there is no art in it. The one secret is to stop when you have finished, naturally and simply. You have reached the climax of your thought or argument. If you have dealt with your subject rightly, you have produced a cumulative impression, built up naturally and inevitably from point to point. The finish is just the last brick put in its place, with that little tap of the mason's trowel to settle it down into position. Do not over-emphasise the tap, or you will split the brick!

Speaking about bricks reminds me of an old custom of German masons which I used to observe in student days at Marburg. When they finish their part of the house-building, the masons tie a freshly cut branch of a tree to a chimney-pot. This for a double reason, I am told—to inform all the world that their job is now finished, and also, from superstition, to invest the 'dead building' with a touch of life! This suggests two ruinous notions of 'finishing' from our point of view. Surely we do not need to tell our people with a flourish that their glad moment has come: the sigh of the next man in the pew may be eloquent enough! And on the other hand, it is ruinous to try to *pin on* a piece of life at the end: the life should have been present all through the work. If it has not been present, there is no glue yet invented that will enable it to stick on, as if it were a natural growth.

Thus, I am glad to think that the ancient art of the Peroration is a dead art, the peroration as a worked up, somewhat artificial, last spasm. People always knew it was coming, and said, 'Now he is in the last lap': or, if they were more dignified, they quoted Cardinal Beaufort, in the second part of *Henry VII*:

> What means this passionate discourse
> This peroration with such circumstance?

Let us take a concrete instance. We have expounded and dealt with some subject in the best and most interesting way possible for us. There only remains, I think, to apply the truth—a principle, a duty, a code of life, or a doctrine—in a natural and practical way, taking care lest in applying it we forfeit the people's interest. When we have applied our truth, what is there more natural than just to stop? Abruptness may be no loss, so long as we do not leave our subject or our people hanging in the air. If you are speaking without paper, prepare your ending more carefully than anything. Get a good ringing sentence, and sit down square on the top of it.

There may be occasions when you do not need what is called an application. Sometimes, it is best to deal with your subject in such fashion that the people will apply it naturally for themselves. Occasionally for this purpose, as I have hinted, abruptness may be the most effective weapon. In any case, try to finish on your best note. A conclusion should be a conclusion, and not only a stop. And apart from all self-conscious art, remember that you are pleading for a verdict, and calling on men and women to turn from sin and commit themselves to God. Everything in the sermon is a means to an end: and it is the end that counts.

When one discusses a subject in this analytical fashion, a young man is more apt to be paralysed than inspired. How can any mastery be commanded, amid so many difficulties? The answer is simple. Mastery is never commanded: it comes naturally in its own time, as a gentle rain. For weeks on end I have watched a little child struggling to walk. During that time there was nothing but blunders and falls, until one day the child, to its own astonishment, suddenly did the impossible—it walked! That is how any mastery or success comes in our work. It is the unexpected fruit of countless failures. Each winter I grow some daffodil bulbs in bowls in my study. I have watched them growing, shooting up their pointed leaves and flower-stalks. And yet, never until the flower naturally expanded, have I caught any hint of scent. Then, in a flash, it arrives like a benediction and sprays my room with fragrance. This is the hope I hold out for all of us who are steadily growing. One day, as the flower opens, *the scent will come!* It is the day of our mastery. But its secret lies deep in the long slow growth of the dark winter.

There is only one excuse and justification for all this talk about the art and craft of preaching—a love for God and a passion for the souls of men, so that we are willing to submit ourselves and our gifts for the invasion of the Holy Spirit. Without the grace of God and a passion for others, the most finished discourse is a tinkling cymbal!

4 The Marks of Good Preaching

The passions are the only orators that always persuade; they are, as it were, a natural art, the rules of which are infallible: and the simplest man with passion is more persuasive than the most eloquent without it. LA ROCHEFOUCAULD, *Maxims*

INTRODUCTION

1. THE MANNER AND THE MATTER

Dr. Guthrie of Edinburgh, a preacher of equal genius and power, used to sum up his advice to students in the following epigram: 'The manner is to the matter as the powder is to the ball.' This crystallises the oft-quoted opinion of Cicero, the prince of speakers, 'To know what we should say, and to know in what order, is indeed a thing of great importance; but to know *how* we must say it, is a thing of much greater importance.' As public speakers, we are concerned not only with the shot, but with getting the shot home. A mere mass of material, however good, and however excellently thought-out and arranged, is not preaching, any more than a heap of ammunition argues a victory. The ammunition of course is a matter of the first rank. But in the last resort, it is the use, good or bad, of this store of shell that decides the day.

So far we have been dealing with the accumulation and arrangement of our material, the distinctive message we are now prepared to use. I turn now to the use of it, and in doing so, I take Dr. Guthrie's saying as my motto, 'The manner is to the matter as the powder is to the ball.'

2. THE WARP AND THE WOOF

Success, so far as human means can command it, lies in the harmony of manner and matter. I am sure that a right study of manner is worthy of all good consideration. One of the points I stressed in an earlier lecture was that every natural gift of mind and every grace of expression can be used, and should be used, for the effect of our preaching. It is criminal for any minister to have undeveloped powers or untried resources. God's work is worth all that a man can give, and worth all the man. If we do use all our powers of expression and thought, then, so far as results are within our reach, we may quote the speech in Addison's *Cato*:

> 'Tis not in mortals to command success,
> But we'll do more, Sempronius, we'll deserve it.

In a true sense, every sermon is only worth the result it produces. Its whole purpose is to effect some influence on the mind, will, conscience and life. In the final issue, it must be judged by this alone and by no other hypercritical standard. No matter how clever or dramatic or learned it be, if a sermon does not effect something for life and character, I do not see that it has any reason for its being. I am quite sure it cannot be judged as something literary or artistic, though both literature and art may have tinged it. It cannot be judged, as Shakespeare judged the drama, by its ability to please or stir admiration, but only by its influence on will and conscience. I say this because we shall now need to discuss some of the literary and artistic qualities that pervade the sermon; but these are only means to an end. Remember, in this as in other things, that if there are arts in preaching, they are necessarily concealed arts. These arts, as some one has said, should be like the human skeleton—there all the time, but decently covered! The moment they become obtrusive or dominating or even merely evident, the power of preaching is lessened: for this turns the thoughts of the people from the message to the messenger—the one unpardonable thing in Christian preaching. Do you remember how Ezekiel sketched this tragedy of the preacher with bitter words—though in his case the fault was the people's, not his—'Lo, thou art unto them as a very lovely song of one that hath a pleasant voice and can play well upon an instrument, for they hear thy words but they do them not.'

You have to consider, then, the manner in which you will serve and handle your material. May I mention first, mainly in order to get rid of them, three defects of personal manner to which an average young preacher is specially liable.

3. THE PREACHER'S PITFALLS

(*a*) *A young man's perilous gift of sarcasm and innuendo.* Sarcasm when fittingly employed is a most effective weapon; but it *is* a weapon, and it wounds. I remember a school teacher who seldom thrashed us except with his tongue: but that tongue left some blisters that never healed. His method seemed merciful compared with other teachers: but really, it was a species of refined cruelty. We school children would much rather have had an honest 'smashing' and been done with it; no decent boy bears a grudge for a plain drubbing. Now, you as ministers occupy a privileged place very similar to the position of that teacher with us. Your people have no right of reply. Their only remedy is a negative one, absence. If we, therefore, in our writing or speech, adopt the dubious means of sarcasm, we may hurt without healing. At the best, this is a futile and irritating gift. It is one of the easiest and cheapest styles to acquire, as any third-rate politician will tell you. There may be occasions when this type of speech comes with apt power, but I think that in any ordinary congregation these occasions are better 'honoured in the breach than the observance'.

(*b*) *The young man's undoubted gift of whole-hearted scolding,* what we in Scotland call 'flyting'. At first—I am impaling my own youth, remember—at first we begin by denouncing sin and flagrant wrong. We do it in the grand manner, with a fine choice anger and whirling words. Wholesale remedies seem easy to young minds. If only older people would stand aside and leave it to us, we could sweep the State clean!

Now, without any doubt, there is room for invective and red anger. Perhaps we are not angry enough. If Jesus walked down our city to-day, I think His eyes would blaze with mingled pity and passion—pity that some have so little, and passion that some have so much. I should like to witness our Lord's royal anger that in this Christian land sin occupies all the strategic corners. The written record of the prophets and Christ's scourging of the Pharisees are commentary enough on that. There are public and private sins that need to be exposed. Perhaps the only way to heal them is to expose them. I daresay any balanced preaching will not miss this strong corrective note. Oddly enough—you will notice this later on—there is a large section of any audience that rather likes to be flayed. Just as some people find a twisted pleasure in melancholy, so there are crowds who like to see themselves and other people in the public pillory. It is a peculiar psychological fact. People call it, generally, 'faithful preaching'.

Just after he retired, Ian Maclaren wrote an article in the *British Weekly* in which he summed up his ministry by saying that if he had it all to live over again, he would preach more comfort. Such a testimony is worth our notice. Though 'flyting' may be good and healthy, it is too fatally easy. All our ministries have been corrupted by it. As the days go by, we realise more and more the struggles of men, the disadvantages under which so many labour, and the load of heredity. Most of all, we realise the buried good that lies in the worst. Years and experience need not make us careless or casual, but they should make us mellow and balanced in judgment. Day by day we see the appalling need of comfort and heartening. And more than that, we learn that comfort and inspiration will do the same work and do it better. In any case, I think old Quaker Penn's bit of wisdom, in the *Fruits of Solitude*, is worth chewing: 'They have a right to censure, that have a heart to help.' If you have John Earle's *Microcosmography* among your books, read his choice essay on 'A Raw Young Preacher', and the following one on 'A Grave Divine'.

(*c*) *No fireworks*. Your business is serious gunfire with a target. Dr. Denney, a master of strong things, used to say to us that no man could exalt himself and Jesus Christ at the same time. It is a terrible thing if people only see us and our 'splash' instead of God's face. There must be personality in every preacher, but that is a different thing from personal display. Cleverness such as this, which in the end only obscures God, may show itself in many subtle ways—in fine writing or fine gymnastics, in literary artificiality or affected ways, in an epigram or a posture. Gentlemen, plenty of fire, but no fireworks!

With these things said, I should like to enquire what are some of the qualities which should distinguish our work, whether it be read or spoken.

CLEARNESS IN PREACHING

Undoubtedly, the first quality we should aim at is *clearness*. People ought to know what we mean. We are preaching presumably to tell them something definite. Have you ever noticed a criticism in the New Testament of our Lord's preaching? It is said that the common people heard Him gladly. In other words, they liked His plain and simple teaching and His direct and helpful illustrations, so different from the obscure and tortuous pedantries of the Scribes and Pharisees.

There are three means to lucidity, which we ought to ensure.

I. CLEAR THINKING

We ought to be clear and exact in our private thinking. If we are not very sure of what we mean ourselves, if we have not grasped our ideas in their range and focus, it is not very likely that other people will. Whatever is shadowy or undefined to us, with blurred edges, will be equally formless to those whom we address.

I do not say for a moment that 'clearness' ensures that you will always be understood. If you are dealing with a high and difficult train of thought or some subtle poetic conception, all the clearness in your own thinking will not make somebody else comprehend it, if he is not thinking on your own plane. For instance, you may be quite clear in an exposition of Kant's view of reality or Bergson's theory of laughter—though I hope you will never be fool enough to speak of these things in a sermon—and yet you may not be understood by the man in the street. But in that case, you have done your best, and the fault is not yours but his. Thus in urging you to make your thought clear, I do not say that you can always make it easy. You cannot break down high thinking into soft pap for children. You cannot make the Atonement of Jesus or Justification by Faith or a doctrine of Immortality or the Election of God *easy*. If there is a thinking mind at one end, there must be a thinking mind at the other.

But see at least that the difficulty in any line of thinking or argument is not due to you. Half-cooked thought is indigestible to others, as well as to ourselves. It is our duty to have as exact and accurate thinking as is within our compass. Beyond that, the rest is with the Spirit of God.

I remember an interview I had with Dr. Whyte of Edinburgh which may illustrate this point. I was under call to go to Broughton Place Church in Edinburgh, and being only twenty-eight years of age at the time, I was shying like a frightened colt. I called to see Dr. Whyte to ask his guidance. He turned to me with his own quick abrupt way, reminiscent somewhat of the peck of a bird, and said, 'Young man, can you clarify your thought?' I answered that

I imagined I could clarify any thought I happened to have. 'Then,' he said, 'you needn't be afraid to follow your predecessor anywhere. That fine man had big moving thoughts, but he could never quite focus them. He was always groping after something that seemed to defy definition. If you can clarify your thought, you can go anywhere.'

I think this clarification of thought should be our first endeavour in preaching. We should have in our own mind, as clear as crystal, what we want to teach and expound. If it be a fine conception with delicate toning and shading, or what the old writers called a 'quaint conceit', give only the more diligence to make the light and shadow clear. Beyond that you cannot go: but so much at least you must assure.

For this purpose of clearness, don't be afraid of *judicious repetition*. If you have any reason to doubt whether your statement is obvious, repeat it in another form or other words, or perhaps in another aspect. An illustration, for instance, may do this finely, if it is apposite. In a public speaker, conciseness is often as great a danger as diffuseness. The more closely reasoned an argument is, the more must you amplify it for the ordinary hearer. If your second position rests on your first, you dare not move until you have made your first position plain. Otherwise, you cannot expect to carry your hearers with you.

2. CLARITY OF LANGUAGE

The second means to clearness is *language*. Words are designed to be our vehicle for thought. They are our intellectual counters, the standard coinage for the exchange of ideas.

Clearness, here, depends on one or two things.

(*a*) Plain simple Anglo-Saxon words, accurately and delicately used. One writer has said that the language of preaching should be 'the language of the market-place and the home raised to its highest power'. Matthew Arnold defines good writing as simple chaste language used with a 'high seriousness'.

It is worth noticing what a fine range of expression there is in ordinary Anglo-Saxon words. I do not wish to impoverish our use of language; and of course the more words, expressions and idioms we have, rightly and delicately used, the finer and the suppler is the sword we wield. But some people, fond of statistics, have reckoned that the 'average man' has only a working vocabulary of a few hundred words at his command. All things considered, it is astonishing how well he can frame his ideas within this limited range.

Further, in speaking to children, remember that their range of words is even more restricted. It is quite useless to attempt to address young people unless we are willing to prune our language to their age and understanding. Not long ago I heard a speaker talking to young people about the 'evolution of an organism'. Now, that is a simple instance of a phrase, a common counter in our adult speech, which is yet hopelessly out of place in addressing young people. Do we realise—it is part of our job that we should—that we must speak on a simple plane to simple people? This is not a suggestion that we should 'come down to their level', as the saying goes. A child's level of understanding, apart from words with which he is not familiar, is astonishingly high. If we can make our ideas simple and clear, and dress them in common ordinary speech, we can speak of many high things to simple people and young children.

But while I am speaking about simple language, may I ask you to consider what a magnificent use can be made of it, by the finest intellectual speakers? If you have any interest in this pressing matter, take two of the most noted speakers whom I can recall at the moment. Read the published speeches of either John Bright or Abraham Lincoln, and you will see what a fine piece of power simple language is in the hands of an expert. Take the famous Gettysburg speech of Lincoln, and you will find what a marvellously plastic thing Anglo-Saxon English can be. Make such simple speaking your model, and your speech will become like words on wheels.

(*b*) It is needful to know the precise meanings of the words we handle. The more we know about words, the finer shadings do we find between them: and language used with delicate mastery is like a rapier in the hands of a fencer. Most of you know a book called a *Dictionary of Synonyms*. The book is a contradiction in terms. There are no synonyms. Words have a life and meaning of their own. You might as well call two brothers synonyms, because they are very much alike. Some of us smile at the common talk about the 'inevitable word': but I am sure it would make for clearness and understanding if we used our words with a finer delicacy. 'Royal thoughts should wear royal robes.'

Barrie tells how Sentimental Tommy once drew public scorn upon himself for want of a word. 'It is so easy, too, to find the right word,' asserted Mr. Gloag, one of the annoyed examiners. 'It's no,' cried Tommy, 'it is as difficult as to hit a squirrel.' A little later, when the young essay-writer had found the elusive word, he thrust his tear-stained face in the door of the room and cried, 'I ken the word now: it came to me a' at once: it is hantle!'

The fine use of language is a joy to the speaker and the audience alike. How may we acquire it? Perhaps Mark Twain's humorous answer is as good as any, 'Read the dictionary.' I have no doubt about the American humorist's meaning—that anyone who knows the *roots* and *ideas* of words will use them finely and exactly, as one handles ancient pottery. I do not advise you to con the dictionary to collect an array of high-sounding words. But as a modern essayist has said, you should widen your vocabulary, 'not that you may use many or large words, but that you may use few, and those few exact for the occasion'.

(*c*) This will result in an application of that art of omission to which I referred in a previous lecture. Highly coloured and meaningless adjectives will die a just death: redundant phrases and ambiguous expressions will be ruthlessly excised: cumbrous and cumulative sentences, which only darken counsel, will be discarded or at least decently chopped up. In the same way, your purple passages will be revised. I do not want to rob anyone of his purple writing, so dear to our vain soul. But it is worth knowing, as a matter of art, that by the plain law of contrast, a purple passage will seem more gorgeously purple, if it is set like a jewel on a simple ring! As a general principle, too much emphasis of any kind, in speaking or in writing, defeats itself. It becomes a monotone, a monotone of emphasis. It is like the young schoolgirl who underlines every second word of her letter. The emphasis becomes so monotonous that she might as well not underline anything at all. In the same way, too much fine writing, purple painting, and literary exaggeration strangle each other. As a principle of art, if you really want to put that purple passage in—if it would actually draw blood from you to cut it out—place it, like a coral island, in a surrounding sea of severe and quiet writing. That is the only way to show up its *rainbow hues*!

I wonder if you ever practise expression apart from the work and exercises which your duties demand. Dr. Forrest, of Glasgow

College, once told me how he trained himself in command of words. I do not remember any one who could talk a subject out—or a man out—so effectively as Dr. Forrest. In spite of this later facility, he told me that as a young man he had felt stilted and hampered in the use of words. Do not smile when I tell you the experiment he employed to give him some mastery. It was evidently serious to him, and it helped to make him the power he was. Each morning, before he started shaving, he chose a sentence from a book, and then during the process of barbering, he tried to recast that sentence into five or six different forms, without altering its meaning. Only, if you try that, use a safety razor!

To balance this, may I counsel you to beware of that command of language which really means that the language has command of us. Some speakers suffer from what one might call a 'verbal flux'. One pointed writer on this subject remarks wittily that many fluent speakers have as much command of language as a driver has of a runaway horse.

3. CLARITY THROUGH ILLUSTRATION

The third main item contributing to clearness is *illustration.* There is no doubt that many people can only grasp ideas when they are put before them in a concrete form. We may regret this. But instead of being impatient with mediocrity, it is our duty rather to deal with it sympathetically. It is certainly easier to get at the average mind by a picture than by an idea. There is a fine Arab proverb which says, 'He is the best speaker who can turn the ear into an eye.'

Some of us are inclined to despise illustration. Perhaps we have had good reason. May Providence shield us from the preacher whose sermon, like a soirée speech, is a string of anecdotes. I have one ministerial friend, otherwise harmless, who is afflicted with this disease. The last time I saw him, he said to me, 'I've got three dandy illustrations, and I am looking for a good text.' That, of course, is the last ditch. Many of us would like to die *before* we reach it!

But it is no condemnation of a good thing that it is often abused. Our criterion for illustration, as for simple speech, may well be the example of our Lord. The proportion of parable and illustration, developed or in germ, throughout the preserved record of our Master's teaching is quite remarkable. This proves two things to my mind—first, the generous use made by Jesus of teaching by illustration and second, the appeal which this method of teaching made to the memory of His hearers. Like most of us, the disciples recalled a parable while they forgot a moral.

In addition to this, you cannot fail to notice the splendid use made of illustration by preachers of power and renown. Chalmers and Guthrie in Scotland, Spurgeon and Maclaren in England, Ward Beecher and Phillips Brooks in America, each man used illustration generously and finely. If only you use it finely, it does not matter so much how generously you use it.

Still, there is a kind of 'philosophy' of illustration. The idea is simply to *illustrate*, or lighten up. An illustration is a window to let in air and light. Hence an illustration that does not illustrate, is worse than useless—it is irritating! The true purpose of illustration is to show the thought or idea *in action*. If it does not do that finely, you are better without it. See therefore that your illustrations are never tawdry or cheap. They may be about common things—the best always are—but they need not be commonplace. In using your illustration, please do not prolong the agony! Avoid all useless or irrelevant details. Sketch your analogy or story quickly and pointedly. The ideal here is the impressionist picture rather than the etcher's detail.

Some young preachers are worried because they realise the value of illustration, but believe they have no gift or faculty for it. I used to feel this myself strongly: and I notice now that my early sermons are as devoid of illustration as a bald man of hair. Then I discovered the lack of it for ordinary preaching, and I have tried to cultivate it ever since. I want to tell you my methods—if by chance they should be of any help.

(*a*) In general reading, if you have that homiletic mind or bias of which I spoke in a previous lecture, you will notice striking things, situations or incidents, and you will see generally how practice illustrates theory. You are reading *Timon of Athens* or *King Lear*. You say 'What a commentary on Ingratitude.' Well, jot it down in your Common-Place Book under that heading.

(By the way, do you keep a Common-Place Book? I use mine most irregularly, worse luck; but I reproach myself sincerely every day for my slackness. I have one like a big business ledger, with printed index at the end, in which, when I remember, I jot down such things as I am commending to you.)

Again, you are reading George Borrow, and you are struck with the misery of the old preacher who thought he had committed the unpardonable sin. You will find no more striking illustration of the exquisite agony of such misguided and unbalanced people than that old parson. Perhaps you are reading Edwin Arnold's *Light of Asia*, and you notice how the King tried to shield the young Buddha from the knowledge of evil, hoping that ignorance would keep him contented. Again, you are reading Hood's *Eugene Aram*, where you have a fierce picture of a guilty conscience. Or you are going through Sir Joshua Reynolds' *Discourses*, and you light on that striking passage where, in spite of preconceptions, he taught himself to love and appreciate Raphael's pictures. If ever you want to illustrate how a man may train himself to love the best things and appreciate them, could you find a more arresting instance? Or you are reading Marlowe's *Dr. Faustus*, and you think of the tragedy of big men using wrong means for good ends, the low road to the high goal. Compare that for instance with the magnificent renunciation of Jesus in the temptation in the Wilderness. Mrs. Gaskell, in her novel *Mary Barton*, tells how Jem, in a dramatic temptation, was rescued from sin by a flashing memory of his mother. Is that worth remembering? Anatole France, in his priceless gem, *The Procurator of Judæa*, shows how a man can be an instrument in the world's destiny, and yet can forget his own past in a soulless service of his lower self. Can you use that for high warning? Perhaps you are re-reading your *Iliad* and you are struck afresh with the passionate figure of Achilles sulking in his tent, the immortal illustration of petty personal rancour defeating the common good. Or you are studying Pliny's *Letters*, which tell as faithfully as Juvenal or Tacitus or Seneca the evil things of Roman Society in the early Empire; but whereas each of the others is bitter and paints pictures which make the modern world shudder, yet Pliny, with his gentle mind, can go through the same evil, see it and handle it, and still preserve balance and sweetness.

I do not think this is mishandling literature or history. May I urge you to go through your books with a noting and claiming eye? Don't seek illustrations: let them find you as you read. I am only amazed at the unused treasure lying at our feet.

At the risk of making this lecture lop-sided and out of joint, I shall go on to speak further about illustration, for if you resemble me, in my College days, you will value another man's experience in this particular.

(*b*) So further, I commend illustration from your own eye. Apart from reading, this is the most fruitful quarter for me, especially in speaking to children. I shall tell you what I do—it is a great secret. *I keep these two eyes as wide open as I can.* That is all. Walter Scott said he learned the secrets of human nature from talking to the man on the driver's box. You do the same. If you see a woodman cutting down trees, talk to him and ask him things. He will never resent it, if he sees you are interested. There are the rings through the sawn tree, the record of its life and growth, stamped there as awesomely as our own growth is graven on our mind and body. He will tell you another interesting thing. I pointed to a tree and said, 'I see the fungus has done that fellow in.' 'No,' he replied, 'fungus never hurts a healthy tree.' Disease always comes first, and then the fungus gets a hold. Can you apply that to life? I talked to a stonebreaker in Jersey one day. He took a piece of flint, and tapped it on this side and tapped it on that. Then he turned it over, and tapped it again smartly twice. When it did not break he took it and pitched it over the hedge. He told me he had given it enough chances. Can you apply that to life, even to God's patience? Have you ever noticed which end of a rose-pole, stuck in the garden, begins to decay first? Is it the upper end, exposed to the severe weathering of sun and frost and rain? or is it the lower end, surrounded by the wet cloggy earth and exposed to its acid actions? The truth is, it is neither! The part that decays first is the line of the pole between the two, just where the earth and the air meet. Does this not give us the secret of all degeneration, most of all among ourselves—when we are neither one thing nor another, neither for nor against? Moderatism, ideal philosophically, is the one thing in this world that is morally unsafe. It has no passions, good or bad, to save it or cleanse it.

I went through the bulb fields of Holland in tulip time, when the flowers in their chequered and garish colours flared in the April sun like an old-fashioned bed-quilt. The little canals leading the water into the sandy soil were crossed by a foot-wide plank. I did not find the adventure difficult, until we came to a canal about four yards wide with only the same narrow plank across. Honestly, I was glad when my wife refused to move. It saved my face! How did we get over? You say, 'Broaden the path of course.' The overseer blew his whistle, and another man came down the opposite side of the canal and handed over a thin pole, which was fitted into an upright on either side, with an arrangement like a 'V' at the top. Then I made a marvellous discovery—how easily you may cross the narrowest plank *if only you have something to hold on to!* Can you apply that to life? Will God broaden the narrow path of duty or temptation for anyone, or will He only give you something to hold on to—perhaps a friend, perhaps Jesus, perhaps only the memory of a loved one?

Well, there you are. Forgive me for such personal talk. But I want you to use your eyes and apply your agile minds, so that your rich experience may become a store-house for yourself and others. There is all the difference, however, between a storehouse and a dungeon.

4. TO QUOTE OR NOT TO QUOTE

Allied with illustration, in this matter of clearness, is the vexed question of *quotation.* As I judge the matter, our object in making a quotation should be either to say something in flashing and memorable words, something that has been perfectly said once for all in classic beauty: or it should be to summon to our aid a competent authority on our subject, whose views are either impressive or final. For these good uses I have no quarrel with the modern habit of quotation in sermons, though I think it is much abused and altogether too profuse. Some sermons remind me of Sir John Lubbock's Essays on *The Pleasures of Life*, which are little more than an array of quotations strung together on a rather nebulous thread. He gives me the impression of having been very busy with his Common-Place Book! But where quotations are used, as they so often are, for mere *ornament*, like pot-plants dotted over a fine stretch of green lawn—and just as artificially and inartistically—a good hearer is annoyed beyond bearing. Some people tell you that they use quotations to lighten up a discourse: but the real question is whether the quotations are *windows* in any sense! I have heard preachers remark, 'as someone has said'—and then I cannot help feeling that what the someone has said wasn't worth saying.

I wonder if I am prejudiced against quotation by Dr. Denney? He stopped in his class one day and said, 'Gentlemen, have you ever noticed that the Apostles seldom quote, except from the sole source of their authority?' At any rate, I am sure that quotation, especially from the poets, is grossly overdone. It gives a fine air and makes some uncritical hearers imagine that the sermon has a literary flavour. Moreover, there is a certain species of person in every audience who simply adores it. He judges the sermon by the number of its quotations!

May I be forgiven two remarks on this vexed question?

(*a*) Some people use quotations as if they were *proofs*. They appeal to what I call 'the fallacy of the big name'. You may hear them say, 'Shakespeare remarks'—as if that settled it! In the first place, it is not always Shakespeare who says it, for Shakespeare was an artist and made his characters think and speak according to character. And so—humbling thought—it is often a fool or a knave who says it! And in the last resort, of course, Shakespeare may be wrong. Even the gods can nod!

(*b*) A quotation, as commonly used, often interrupts the line of progress and argument. You perhaps want one line or phrase in the quotation, but to use that, you may have to quote a whole verse. I have noticed in listening to people quoting, that the speaker has often to 'catch up' the audience again, where his quotation interrupted. Generally, I would say, a quotation should come as if it were inevitable: and often, where it is inevitable it is better left alone. It is certainly better left alone where it is hackneyed and fly-blown. I shall have served my purpose if I make you disagree with me, and so lead you to examine the matter for yourselves. After delivering this lecture in Aberdeen, I received a letter from Sir George Adam Smith, Principal of the University, in which he said, 'I am glad you have touched on the question of quotations in sermons. In my experience of listening to sermons, no art is more difficult than that of using relevant quotations. The most of those I have heard distract the hearer from the main theme of the discourse.'

I promised you that this lecture would be lop-sided, and I am keeping my promise. However, it is not as lop-sided as it seems, for I am certain that the general question of clearness, which I have been emphasising, is so important that it would justify a serious discussion.

However, I wish to speak very briefly about a few other qualities of a sermon.

DIRECTNESS AND POINTEDNESS

I advise you to preach like fencers with the foils off. General vague speaking never touches anybody. As hearers, we think it applies to the man in the next pew! I do not see why we should not try to strike home. In *A Priest to the Temple*, George Herbert remarks that the ideal preacher always comes to a point where he can say, 'This is for you, and this is for you', and adds 'particulars ever touch and awake more than generals'. Nathan spoke to David a choice little parable about a ewe lamb, and David was charmingly indignant! It was a different matter when Nathan pointed the finger direct, and said, 'Thou art the man.'

Now a sermon or a message can be swamped in generalities, however true. I do not see why we should not be direct and pointed, both in manner and matter. It need not be a question of a big bludgeon, smashing people and beating them down. There is such a weapon as a rapier, and even the household pin! I think we can get nearer home, even by the pronouns we choose. In an essay one uses such forms as these, 'It is said', 'It is commonly reported', 'Public opinion believes', 'There is a prevalent idea', and so on—the suggestion being that an essay should be impersonal. But speaking, in its very idea, is personal. I do not see why we should not be more direct, so long as we are not rude or individual. Why don't we say, 'Some of us here', 'If any of you challenge this, what then?' or 'I at least am convinced'. If some of the writers I have read on this subject are correct, then preaching is, first and last, a *testimony*, a testimony of the Church's faith and ours, or rather the Church's faith made ours. Let us testify, then, by all means! I do not want you to use the personal pronoun too much, but still be direct, and straight, and frank, and pointed. I am struck by the fact, in reading great speeches, even political speeches, that the big moment of power comes when the orator says, 'I appeal to you.'

The same applies, of course, to the form of speech as well as to the matter. It is worth remembering what Matthew Arnold, himself a great purist in writing, says about a direct style. 'Style! Style! what is all this talk about style? I do not know anything about it, except that a man should have something to say and then say it as briefly as possible, in language suited to the occasion.'

BEING ONESELF

I believe in the *Need of Naturalness.*

> I seek divine simplicity in him
> Who handles things divine.

Why is it, when a man goes into the pulpit, that he seems to become somebody else. He acquires a drone or a whine, at least an unnatural voice and manner, as if he had adorned himself with it in the vestry along with his robes. Perhaps it is from a sense of dignity or solemnity, or an overwhelming feeling of awe. If so, it does not convey that impression to the audience. The average natural man nowadays feels that we have a professional manner, and he does not like it. Now I have no desire to lessen the dignity or the solemnity of preaching and worship, but I fail to see that we need be stilted or unnatural in manner or voice to achieve this. When Ezekiel fell down in unmanly prostration before the Spirit's call, a voice said, 'Son of man, stand upon thy feet.' God speaks to us only in the exercise of our natural manhood.

In speaking to sensible Christian young men to-day, you will find that this is their main complaint against ministers. They meet us socially and find that we speak and laugh like ordinary mortals, and yet in the pulpit we have a 'manner and voice', a voice that seems to come from our toes. To begin with, it is not good speaking. Good speaking is always natural and easy. Further, it is not good policy, for it makes religion seem unnatural, as if it were a mode of thought and expression which we assume for the time, and then lay aside when worship is over. Our task to-day is to show people, especially young people, that religion is human nature in all its natural bigness, glorified and perfected in Jesus Christ, and that Jesus does not limit or starve the manhood and womanhood which is God's gift to us. Therefore I say, even for the dignity and praise of religion, you do better in the long run to err on the side of naturalness than on the side of stiffness. Cultivate the easy good graces of any gentlemanly speaker. Try to be at your ease without being cheap, and speak in the natural voice God has given you, trained by the laws of decent voice production. Moreover, if you speak naturally and easily with an open throat, you can speak at countless meetings without physical strain.

A MAN ON FIRE

Professor Stuart Blackie once came to Glasgow to address the students of his year on this subject of preaching. One memorable sentence was this, '*A preacher is a man with a message, on fire.*' My next point about the needed qualities of preaching is to emphasise the two words 'On Fire'. It is the message, burning in our own heart, that begets the heat. We are in dead earnest, and earnestness creates enthusiasm and passion. 'He who is near me is near fire.' I once had an assistant who preached a helpful sermon. Afterwards, in my own house, he foolishly invited my criticism. I could not criticise the material of the sermon, for it was rich and finely flavoured with his own peculiar experience, but I asked him if he believed what he had preached. Rather indignantly he replied, 'Yes, of course.' 'Well,' I answered, 'you spoke as if it might have been a page out of Charles Lamb.'

One is reminded of the famous reply of Garrick, the actor, to the Bishop who asked him how he as an actor could produce such a magical effect on an audience by the representation of fiction. Garrick replied (I quote from memory), 'Because I recite fiction as if it were truth, and you preach truth as if it were fiction.' Why should we not have Jeremiah's ideal—'His word was in mine heart as a burning fire shut up in my bones, and I was weary with forebearing and I could not stay.' Preaching lit at such a fire is a real torch.

If preaching is in any sense testimony, testimony of the saving grace of Jesus and the love of God, let us do it with at least the natural warmth and interest with which we would testify for the character of a friend. I do not want heat where there should be no heat. Dr. Denney is reported to have criticised a student's sermon as an instance of 'heat without light'. But where there is light, there is heat of some kind, the natural warmth that light imparts.

THE SOUL OF WIT

Lastly, *few sermons ever err by brevity*. I received a copy of the letter in which Mr. Warrack announced his desire to found the Warrack Lectureship in Scotland. In it he makes special reference to the need of brevity, and asks the lecturer to refer particularly to this requisite of good preaching. I do not refer to it only because he asked me, though I admit that the opinion of any intelligent layman on this question is well worth having. This reminds me of the tale of the man who was narrating very eloquently all the hardships the Pilgrim Fathers had to endure—the troubles, anxieties, and cares they had to put up with. Some one asked him, 'But what of the Pilgrim Mothers?' The man replied, 'But what specially had they to put up with?' 'Oh,' replied the other, 'with the Pilgrim Fathers.'

Now, I do not think lay opinion, *which has to put up with us*, is unreasonable. If any one of us is interesting and grips the people's attention, we shall find that our audience will not judge us by the hour-glass. But we live in an age that loves compression, the age of the magazine article: and unless we are extraordinarily gifted, people are not prepared to take from us what they will not take from anyone else. We should learn to get our message within its natural compass. Our sermons need not be like these lectures of mine, subject to a prescribed time-limit, a set time to be fully used and yet not exceeded! We should preach according to our subject and not according to the clock. If the subject demands a limited treatment, stop. If your people come to know that you preach by your subject and not by so many pages, then when you have a big subject, they will not grudge the extra time. But so far as most of us are concerned, ordinary mortals, we never err by conciseness and brevity. Henry Drummond, a fascinating speaker if ever there was one, is reported to have said that he could undertake to hold an audience for twenty minutes, but not for twenty-one. This may seem extreme, but it expresses a fine truth.

We should try to leave our people with an appetite for more, not 'stodged', as the schoolboy puts it, but decently hungry.

5 The Use of our Material in Preaching

Alas for the unhappy man that is called to stand in the pulpit, and not give the bread of life.

EMERSON

INTRODUCTION

I. THE BIBLE AS OUR SOURCE

The accepted source of our preaching material is the Bible. It is the official record of our religion, of God's dealings with man, and man's experience of God. It is the Revelation of God's heart to us, spoken in word and act, down the ages. It is our one authentic record of Jesus and His teaching, and the institution of the Church. Our religion definitely owes its origin to it, is nourished by it, and continually turns back to it for inspiration and correction. Thus it is at once our source and our touchstone of truth.

I emphasise this for two reasons.

(*a*) In our preaching, can we legitimately choose our texts and subjects elsewhere than the Bible? Many have done so, a few with marked power. Dr. Whyte of Edinburgh often chose his subjects from varied religious sources, from Bunyan and the notable saints of the Church. But exceptions apart—for whom of course there is no law—I question if this is either needful or desirable. This seeking of other streams is generally the mark of secondary minds, who imagine that whatever is *outré* is also original. In any case, why go to derivative sources when we have the primitive spring undefiled in our own garden? There is something wrong with the preacher who cannot find at least his jumping-off place in the Bible. The amazing richness and variety of this book are only adequately realised the more it is studied and used. Week by week, we discover new reaches and unguessed horizons, God with the light on His face, and man in his mingled shame and glory. The Bible is as old as God and as new as sin.

(*b*) The need to keep ourselves to the Bible is enforced by the fact, which you will discover more and more in your later ministry, that the book is becoming increasingly unknown and misunderstood. The day of Bible knowledge, as our fathers understood it, is quite gone—a loss that may entail deeper consequences in national life and outlook than any of us yet comprehend.

In one way, preaching was a relatively easy thing in those bygone days. Apart from the fact that variety—the modern minister's bogey—was less needed or expected, one could always presume on a common ground of knowledge and interest between oneself and the audience. The voice in the pulpit awoke an intelligent response in the pew. I am afraid one cannot, at least dare not wisely, presume on that now. Hence there is an untold gain, for the Church and for religion, in any true expounding preaching which makes the Bible and its message its one basis.

2. THE PREACHER'S PROBLEM

The Bible, then, is the source of our preaching material. Our problem is how we may use its varied supply so that we enrich our people with its message, and also make it at the same time a book to which they can turn with understanding, profit and some affection.

This suggests other questions.

(*a*) Using the Bible as our basis, how are we to select our subjects? Are we to graze over the book as a horse grazes aimlessly over a meadow, wandering from tuft to tuft as fancy lures it? If so, much of our field may be uncropped. Or can we have any system or plan by which we can open up the developing truth of the book and reveal not choice tit-bits, but 'the whole counsel of God'? A man-making ministry must have some of this sweep and range about it. Big men are not fed on chance texts.

(*b*) We have a duty, I think, to do this book justice, to make it understood to the modern age, and to give it some place equal to what it had in days gone by, when it welded the character and tempered the conscience of great nations, none more so than our own. If our religion owns this book as its source and inspiration, it is a double folly on our part to think we can keep either religion or the Church living, if the book itself be dead and neglected. When the Bible is put on the shelf, the Church will surely follow it.

(*c*) I believe also that if we reverted to some true and useful form of systematic Bible teaching, we should receive a distinct welcome from the people. I know one thing at least—our more thoughtful young people are keen to understand this book in its modern bearings and implications. I once asked Professor Welch from New College to address my Young People's Society on some Old Testament topic. He simply chose a passage and spoke of it in arresting commentary. At the end of the meeting I was brave enough to ask the young people to vote on what style of preaching they preferred from Sunday to Sunday. Without any hesitation, they 'plumped' for an exposition like Professor Welch's. I admit, of course, that it was Professor Welch! But the point is, *if exposition is well done, it is always acclaimed.* Let us see, so far as we can, that it is well done.

Exposition then pays the people and it pays us. On the one hand, it makes this book a living and real thing for the congregation, a vivid record of human struggles toward God, souls sinning but winning, not a mausoleum of mummies. And on our part as preachers, it saves us from scrappy work where we dance from text to text like summer midges, patronising only our own pet subjects and angular views, and omitting the full circle of Christian truth.

Let me begin then to-day with our use of books and passages, and pass later to subjects, characters and texts. I give the treatment of books and passages first place, because this most of all has fallen into modern disuse and even disrepute.

HOW TO USE A BOOK

Suppose we desire to preach about or through a book, how may we best proceed with our task? Please understand that what I advocate represents only my own view, and you are at full liberty to treat my remarks as you like, or as you think they deserve.

I. HOW NOT TO USE A BOOK

First—how *not* to treat any book!

Many years ago there came to my native town a new minister. He announced that for consecutive teaching, he would speak at the morning service from the book of Philippians. We loved the man for many things: but in the end *we hated the book of Philippians!* When our sincere and beloved minister died, a year and ten months after his induction, he was only in the middle of the second chapter! Now I am not criticising the man—far from it, he was deeply respected—but I am criticising the method. To take a verse, or even a phrase, or often only one word in a verse, and to go unweariedly but wearyingly on, is to make any book a dead thing—not only dead, but worse, detested.

As a general principle, no two books should be treated alike, or by any one method, for the simple reason that no two books *are* alike, either in origin, plan, or purpose. Study your book first, getting its drift and purpose, and then see for yourself how you can best treat it.

2. SOME SUGGESTED METHODS

(*a*) *Expounding by problems.* Some books, I think, can be best expounded round the problems they face, those problems they were written to solve. Instead of commenting on passages as they follow each other in verse and chapter—by the way, wipe out verses and chapters—take the problems which rear up their heads from out of the words, and make them your method of progress and your basis of discussion. I think, for example, that the Epistles to the Church at Corinth can be most usefully expounded for congregational purposes under this mode of treatment. The Apostle wrote these letters to face these questions. In one sense, these problems were the sole reason of his writing. I think therefore they should form the natural scheme of treatment and progress.

As an introduction, you might bring the Apostle into the city. Sketch vividly what he and the young church had to face and endure, the problems of a great commercial centre in ancient days, which are very much the problems of any big seaport to-day, a magnet for roving and hot-blooded men. You could picture the beginning and growth of the young church, with any special difficulties or dangers the Apostle himself had to encounter. From the heterogeneous composition of the new church, you could show further how the problems themselves developed, as they evolve naturally with us, especially in heathen lands. There is no reason why this introductory talk should not be arresting, informative and vividly interesting.

From this, in your next sermon, I should propose that you begin to tackle the varied problems with which the Apostle's letter deals. You will find, I promise you, that they are living questions to-day.

State each in its own range and compass: exhibit what each meant for the people concerned: reveal the dangers threatened to the early church: and state the Apostle's big solution. I predict that each problem will have its blazing counterpart in modern life, and you will not be lashing a dead horse. What could be more modern, say, than the problem of the weak brother—liberty in conscience—going to law—separation from evil—marriage and divorce—how to be reconciled, and a dozen other pressing matters? Under a mould like this, you can group the relevant passages together, and in a few connected yet separate addresses, exhibit a good part of the contribution of the book towards Christian thinking. And above all, you can show that it is a living letter for living men.

(*b*) *Expounding by vices.* Again, another book can be expounded under the sins which it scourges. As a sample of this, one might take the book of Amos. Here we have a great arraignment of a people for its national follies. We have a magnificent opening in the picture of Amos himself, his work and vision, and the greedy, tortuous national life into which he was unexpectedly plunged. For modern political cleansing and the teaching of God about national righteousness, could you have a finer setting than this prophet's mission? Take his message under the sins which it scourges, and show the remedies of a true religion—national greed and selfishness, the oppression of the poor, faithless living, the fallacy and tragedy of apparent prosperity, the penalty of luxury, the decay of public virtue, the appearance without the reality of religion. If you desire to speak to the modern man about national purity, can you have a finer platform? Under a scheme like that, you may unfold the robust message of Amos and relate it clearly to our worried life and our worrying problems.

(*c*) *Expounding by leading ideas.* Again, you may treat another type of book by selecting its leading ideas and making these the links in your chain. These ideas stand out like peaks from the flat land, and by flitting from one to another you can give a fair sketch of the 'geography' of the book. In an epistle like that of James, where the author frequently turns back on his own tracks and reiterates his thoughts under a new guise, I believe that by selecting and relating his principal ideas, you can open up the book in a short strong series. Take his ideas, grouping them together from various passages—on temptation, on works, on ostentation, on purity, on God's providence, on charity, on faith-healing. These things are modern enough in all conscience. Let the Apostle lead you out naturally into these big fields.

I should say, for instance, that this is the only way to make any use, other than mere scraps, of a book like Proverbs. Here, as you know, from the very form and idea of ancient 'wisdom-literature', you have gems scattered in delightful disorder, like the plunder-box in *Treasure Island*. What I suggest is *that you try to string some of the loose jewels together*. Collect a group of proverbs that refer to the same topic. (Professor Foster Kent, by the way, has done this for you in a convenient little book. Under headings, you have the stray proverbs duly classified.) When you have done this, you will find some suggestive material which can be effectively used under heads like these—the teaching of the book about nations and rulers, about the duties of citizens, about wealth, about the family, about usary, about national righteousness, about the rewards of good and the penalties of evil, about the seduction of the streets, about slander. One can easily imagine the interesting groupings, very relevant to modern life, under which you can gather the scattered wisdom of such a practical book. And with an introductory talk about the ancient wise men and their ways, about the schools and teaching of that time, about oral tradition and the marvel of a trained memory—what Roger Ascham calls 'the only key and keeper of all learning'—I do not see why you should not make that book fascinating to your people. In any case, I have found that it made an admirable course of study for a Bible class.

(*d*) *Expounding by events*. Again, for a short course—by the way, avoid long courses: they weary the people and they weary you—for a short course, to open up a book like the Acts of the Apostles, I should suggest treating it under the idea of *the cities into which Paul entered*. In each case you have a fine setting to begin with, a pictorial background that engages interest, a fascinating and turbulent history, and a set of pressing problems. You can bring the Apostle in along the great Roman roads, limping weariedly, dust-laden in the Eastern twilight, and show how he fared. You can exhibit striking instances of the grace of God in each city. You can show, if need be, the future progress of the church which he founded. This scheme with its changing setting is as full of incident as a modern film.

(*e*) *Expounding by portraits*. Or you can treat the same book under another idea—a portrait gallery, types of people whom the disciples met, most of them engaging or at least arresting personalities, men and women in whom the common passions of our heritage ran like red blood. Just consider any half-dozen of them for a moment, with their infinite diversity—Simon Magus, Gamaliel, the Ethiopian Eunuch, Cornelius, Lydia and Festus. They are as different, and yet as typical, as any batch of human characters ever portrayed. Above all things, this is a book of people, not 'acts': and as you know, we are most helped by a study of other stumbling souls. While there is a connected scheme in your mind, one incidental gain will be that each sermon, though related, will be like the proverbial tub, standing on its own bottom.

(*f*) *Customs and Institutions.* Again, an explanation of a book like Deuteronomy or Numbers might be comprised under an exposition of the laws which were promulgated for the Jews, and the institutions which were set up or sanctioned for life and safety. Try a few connected sermons on such topics as these—the ancient law of hospitality, the Cities of Refuge and what they stood for, the provision for the poor, the rights of the gleaners, the harvest laws, the stranger within the gate. You will be able to show at least that these books are unique in their own age for their doctrines of ancient mercy. I think when you have finished a few sermons on such institutions and customs, your people will know in some part the purpose and meaning of the legal books.

(*g*) *Jesus at the cross-roads.* It is much more difficult to suggest a scheme for the Gospels, unless you wish to take the main incidents, developments and crises of Christ's life. You are dealing with big moving topics when you speak of the Baptism, the Temptation, the Break with Tradition, Peter's avowal, Christ's retreats, Bethany, Gethsemane, and the Last Days.

For many years, at Communion seasons, I have always dealt with some incident in Christ's last week. There is material for a man's whole ministry, at the Lord's Table, in these few last crowded days of the Lord on earth.

You may use the Gospels, of course, to give separate and yet related addresses on Christ's teaching under its main categories and divisions, e.g. His teaching about the Kingdom. Or you might provide a useful series on Christ's teaching about *common things*—money, work, home, marriage, duty, pleasure, anger—connecting together the relevant passages.

In any case, if you are doing this type of work, I suggest such pegs as I have described, posts to mark the way. I do not see any other useful fashion in which this desirable exposition of truth can be done for the modern congregation. I feel that we need it, if the Bible is to be understood and used, and especially if it is to remain in any sense the touchstone of our thinking.

(*h*) *Expounding by natural grouping.* Exposition of a more detailed kind can only be done under one plan. It is foolish to take a passage, and as John McNeil once said, 'if pursued in one verse, flee to another'. If you are planning to go through a book, *get the progressive thought into its natural groupings.* There are periods —links and advances—in the Apostle's thinking, as well as in your own. Take this grouping as it suggests itself, and get its central burden. Show what each means, how the writer develops it, its implications and principles, and its fresh application to our Christian life. Avoid burdensome and trivial side-issues and qualifications. Say to yourself, 'Here is the germ of the Apostle's mind and the burden of his teaching.' Open that out generously, as the natural grouping of the passage suggests itself.

Now I do not know whether anything I have said so far is of the slightest use to you, but I am convinced that this type of expository preaching, if well done, has a big place in educating the modern Christian Church. But above all things, realise that it must be done well! The bigger your canvas, the finer must be your grouping and colouring. Some people imagine that a passage is an easy thing to deal with—the sort of sermon a preacher can turn out quickly, when hard-pressed, for he has more 'elbow-room' to walk about in it. He certainly has a good range and freedom of movement: and when well used, that range and horizon may be an element of power and attraction with an audience. But generally it has been this idea of exposition being easy that has been its ruin in the past. I should advise you to give as much diligence and pains, as much or more proportion and poise, as much good writing and clear thinking, to this type of work as to any.

3. THE REWARDS OF EXPOSITION

There are two gains in this type of work which I shall stop to mention.

(*a*) You will take your people through vistas of Christian truth that you might otherwise miss. Other churches have a distinct pull over us in their prescribed passages for reading and sermon, their 'Church Calendar'. We have the privilege, delightful yet perilous, of picking and choosing. Often a man's ministry is made lame, not by his positive preaching *but by the subjects which he deliberately or unwittingly avoids.* I remember once being startled by an old elder informing me that I had never preached on Christian assurance. A little later, in facing a passage of a book, I was brought face to face with this neglected aspect, which I called, 'The grounds of Christian confidence.' So there is this to be said for some systematic treatment of Scripture—that willy-nilly you are made to 'box the compass' and deal with the whole wide circumference of useful truth. This is good for your people, and it is good for you.

(*b*) It is especially good for you in this way. I have not tackled a book yet in my present charge, but for the three previous years I took a book each winter. I found this—it gives a splendid feeling of wealth just to experience it—that after I had gone through the book, I could, if I cared, have turned back and preached on fifty different texts and subjects that stood up by the way and hit me. Even if you only want 'fine texts', this is the best preparation.

PREACHING DOCTRINE

I pass now to say a few words about preaching doctrine. The very mention of this word scares people, chiefly because they think it implies something dry-as-dust. There is no doubt it can be made as 'dry as sand', and as entertaining! But if we remember that doctrine is only truth, stated and arranged, it need not be any more fearsome than other forms of truth. In any case, whether we will or no, *we do preach doctrine, disguised or otherwise.* A man cannot have a faith without having some statement or definition of it.

One objection urged against preaching doctrine is that our faith is a little more fluid than it used to be, with more scope for individual differences. But, surely, even a fluid can be put into convenient vessels for purposes of handling. In spite of those who, in Bacon's phrase, 'count it a bondage to fix a belief', it lies with us as preachers to state the things that are most surely believed.

I am sure we can gain by giving plain talks on doctrine. In an earlier lecture I have expressed my own conviction that we lose by assuming our doctrines to be known and accepted. We assume that people know about the 'Fatherhood of God' and its implications. Do they? We assume that they know what 'forgiveness of sin' is. Do they? We assume that they know what we mean by saying that Jesus 'saves' from sin. Do they? I am convinced that what we have to do is to explain and expound the very truths that we generally assume! For the life of the Church, these are ruinous assumptions.

A Society in Edinburgh University asked four or five of us ministers to come and talk to them. The questions they asked us to discuss were precisely the questions I have mentioned. The subject prescribed to me for instance was, 'What does Christ save us from?' Now, if University men are anxious to know what we mean by the common terms of our faith, you may take it that the average man would value some clear, simple statement, expressed in modern ways and modern terms. I do not know whether you can do this in the regular, more formal guise of a sermon. But even if you cannot, this will only add to interest and variety. I should advise a plain frank talk, perhaps on a Sunday evening, on some of the broad doctrines of our faith. If they are explained in simple language, and where possible, illustrated, I think you will find your reward.

You will notice that I said 'on a Sunday evening'. Later, you will discover that you can count on a 'carry' and interest on a Sunday evening, which you cannot command at a more formal service. There is a natural unbending both on your part and the people's. Use that helpful atmosphere wisely.

In dealing with a doctrine, don't dissect it as if it were a corpse, some dead thing outside yourself which you regard only with intellectual curiosity, but use it as 'the body of our faith' by which we live. As Coleridge remarks, '*Our greatest mission is to rescue admitted truths from the neglect caused by their admission.*' Let us show that our beliefs are real and living, expressing the gathered hopes and dreams of the people of God. 'Belief consists in accepting the affirmations of the soul.' Let us show, in Emerson's phrase, that they *are* the affirmations of the soul!

Generally, in treating doctrinal subjects, translate theology into religion, and the abstract into the concrete. Avoid especially played-out phrases and old shibboleths, once good coin to those who minted them, but now out of common currency. And in speaking on dogma, is there any need to be 'dogmatic'? That annoys, especially from the pulpit, where there is no opportunity for reply. Above all things, bring your doctrine into modern life and translate it into modern terms. Generally, the pulpit is too remote. Any young man, in frank moments, will leave you in no doubt about that.

PREACHING SUBJECTS

A word about subjects.

I had a dreadful experience during my first few months as a minister, which I may use as a warning for you. Like most young men, I knew very little about the business of preaching. I had only about a dozen sermons in my possession, twelve rather dud cartridges in my locker. Here is what I said to myself each week. 'Go to, Sir! thou shalt write a sermon on Temptation'—which I did, dealing with it, in a young man's large way, as comprehensively as I could. I then found a text for it, and tagged it on like a label. And after that, I had absolutely nothing more to say about Temptation! Next week I said, 'Go to, Sir! thou shalt write a sermon on Providence'—which I did, again exhausting the subject as thoroughly as I could. And after that, I had nothing more to say about Providence! . . . And I tell you frankly, at the end of three months, I thought I had exhausted all available truth: and certainly I had exhausted myself. I remember wondering whether I could slink away decently, or whether there should be a public exposure in Presbytery!

Then I made the remarkable discovery, remarkable for me, that if I were only content to preach from a definite text or passage, with its own definite aspect, I could preach on temptation this morning, and temptation the next morning, and temptation the third morning. For I discovered that if I stuck to my passage and dealt with the phase of truth enshrined in it, I could take a dozen texts on temptation, and yet be fresh on each one of them. In attempting to crush a whole subject into one sermon, I was only attempting the impossible, spoiling the subject by unnatural compression, dazing the uncomplaining people, and ruining my own peace and nerves.

So I would say to you at the beginning of your ministry—*do not take subjects, unless for special purposes.* Take your chosen passage or text or incident, and deduce from these premises your conclusion and message. In the long run, it is a richer way. Most of all, it saves you from giving only your own semi-digested views on a big topic, without reference to the touchstone of Biblical truth. If you are dealing with a subject, find the appropriate passages where it is unfolded, and work outwards from them.

When you do have a subject in hand, build as a mason builds, stone on stone. Advance from position to position, with the cumulative effect of remorseless logic, never forgetting, of course, that there is a logic of the heart as well as a logic of the head. State your subject clearly, not shunning any inherent difficulties or gliding gracefully over thin ice. If a man knows you are doing that, you are ruined! Exhibit clearly your steps of progress, making sure that there is no yawning hiatus or unproved assumption. From start to finish, head straight for your conclusion, so that when it comes, it seems an inevitable and sure thing that fastens on a man's conscience and will. Such a conclusion, driven home without escape, may make an appeal more effective than sloppy rhetoric. If you care to apply it, you may: but I have known diffuse applications that only dissipated a tremendous effect. The finest finish is just to show that such and such a conclusion and such and such a decision are *inescapable*.

PREACHING ON CHARACTERS

Use characters and character-studies fairly frequently. For one thing, this gives occasion for a different type of sermon, and anything that lends variety is a source of power. An incident in a man's life provides a fine point of contact with your audience. Generally, I think this type of preaching should be done pictorially, with some imaginative treatment, and in a dramatic setting. It is a piece of life, a film from the world's big drama. Treat it as such, with all the pictorial power you have. Sketch your situation as if you were painting it. Remember here the old Arab proverb, and make 'the ear the eye'. In any dramatic situation, you can make the people *see*.

One point, I think, should be remembered. The Bible generally tells the story or sketches the man's deeds, without any comment. But the sketching is so sure that comment is fairly plain and obvious. Do not let it be too obvious. I heard the President of a

College preach from a dramatic incident in the life of Moses, and then announce his three heads thus:

(1) Moses was a great man.
(2) Moses was a wise man.
(3) Moses was a good man.

So thoroughly true, that everybody had seen it for himself years ago in the Sunday school!

But sometimes the Bible does make a comment or judgment, and I want to warn you about it. This book is so passionately interested in good and evil, that it sees these things clearly as either white or black. You will not find any tonings or fine shadings, any dull gray or neutral brown, about the Bible's judgments. I daresay, in the best sense, a clear and perfect mind does see good and evil as clear white and black. To a perfect judgment, a thing is either good or bad—and that is all that is to be said about it. But we never see it thus, and the average man in the audience never does. The book of Chronicles, for instance, sums up a man's life in two variations of one phrase. 'He did good' or 'he did evil in the sight of the Lord'. But the truth to us may be that he did both good and evil! In dealing with characters always deal with them *as characters*, whether you think they represent men or the nation. This should never be forgotten. Take Saul or Samson. It used to be considered right to pass a sweeping judgment on these two men, and at the end, after you had pummelled them sufficiently, you laid them out on the ground as utter failures. But historical methods have shown us that we cannot do that to-day. We cannot help noticing the shadings of good and evil, if we are dealing with them as bone of our bone. Show your characters, therefore, in all the touches of their humanity, which makes them akin to us in our mingled good and evil. The more you can take them off their pedestal and reveal them in their human weakness and strength, the more appeal do you make to your audience. A plaster saint never helps anybody! But a struggling, sinning, and conquering man always does. Without doubt, this is the reason why an average audience never wearies of Simon Peter—simply because he is sketched in the New Testament in fuller strength and weakness than anybody else. He at least is a struggling, sinning, cursing, weeping and conquering man. Show your big characters, then, as men like ourselves, who by grit and grace, have won through. There is a big appeal there.

In this connection, what about a series which you might call 'An apology for rogues'? What can be said for those who play the villain in the dramas of the Bible—Cain, Achan, Gehazi, Esau, Judas and Demas? Are they all black or all white? That is all I want to suggest to you. Treat them as tempted and sinning men, not as in the old days, as devils hot from hell. I heard a minister discussing that dramatic but shady scene where Jacob tricked Esau of his birthright. All through the sermon he spoke about Jacob as the 'saint'. Now Jacob may have become a saint—after much discipline! But the use of the term, in that particular instance, was distinctly *proleptic*!

HOW TO USE TEXTS

Finally, I wonder if you will welcome a few hints from me about texts?

(*a*) In using a text, be sure that it is not really a concealed passage. In other words, it may not explain itself without its relevant context. An instance may be helpful—only I pray again that I may not be at sea in my exegesis!

I have heard two different sermons on the great text, 'Come unto Me all ye that labour and are heavy laden, and I will give you rest.' Both preachers concentrated at the end, quite rightly, on the *quality* of the rest Christ offered to the world's heavy-laden. But I hold—perhaps I am wrong—that this gift of Jesus is explained only in the remainder of the passage, 'Take My yoke upon you', etc. As we know, there are two kinds of yokes, the yoke that binds the slave to his work, holding him relentlessly there, and the kindly yoke that binds the oxen so that they can work in harmony, pull together, and do their common job in unison and easy mastery. In using the term, therefore, Christ shows precisely what His offer of rest is, not idleness, nor relief, nor slumber, but a gracious yoke, with Himself in the traces beside us, to give us help and courage in facing our duties. Thus it is the idea of the *yoke* which alone explains the promised rest, making it manly and heroic. In a case like that, it is your duty to make sure that your text is not a concealed passage, needing something further to explain it and give it body.

(*b*) Following that out, may I ask you also to beware of any text that is quite evidently only a very limited part of the truth?

I know that you cannot expect to make a sermon a neat little packet of tabloid theology. You should be content, as a general rule, to deal with the special aspect of the truth your text exploits. But where there is a very obvious corollary, it is much better to group complementary texts together, so that the people may have a satisfying view of your subject. For instance, if you wish to speak of human burdens and burden-bearing, why not group these texts together?—'Every man shall bear his own burden', 'Bear ye one another's burden', and 'Cast thy burden upon the Lord'. The first emphasises the place and need of personal grit and courage, the second the duty and function of human sympathy, and the third the inspiration of our faith. In the three you have a wide view.

Or perhaps, a distinct contrast may serve your purpose, and evoke interest and surprise. You announce as your text, 'Remember ye the former things of old', and you announce as your second text, 'Remember ye not the former things of old'. Both sentences relate to the place that a great past may have in our present life, one as a noble and moving inspiration, the other as a smug and ignoble source of content. And in the two, from their respective contexts, you have a balanced view of the use and abuse of memory. See then, while you do not labour for a foolish completeness, that your text does not need some obvious complement or contrast.

(*c*) Do not scour the Bible, as with a small tooth-comb, for out-of-the-way texts. On the other hand, if you strike one, do not despise it. To have a fine situation given you, a unique setting, is often half the battle. You engage interest from the start. In an ideal sense, a text is a jumping-off place, and sometimes, though it is only a diving springboard, it may justify itself if it lets you swim out into the ocean. So long as you do not mutilate a text, chopping it with a hatchet, shearing it off at some catchy but quite impossible place, or so long as you do not twist it out of its one and only meaning, I think you can use many a strange setting. Nowadays, remembering our reservations, we believe it is an absolute Godsend to get something that arrests and holds from the beginning. Take with this, of course, the advice I offered in an earlier lecture, to preach on the big 'sappy' texts and the body-building subjects of our faith. It is a false pride however that makes you neglect a striking setting.

(*d*) Allied with this is a question that affects some of our popular preachers. Have we any right to take a text and 'spiritualise' it—isn't that the phrase?—which means that we use the text merely as a motto? I daresay a good many helpful and useful things may be said under this method. But might not they be said as fittingly under something more appropriate? I should not care to condemn or ban anything that has proved helpful. But the practice is a clear misuse of a text. It is much better to say your nice helpful things without any text at all!

(*e*) You will notice that it is generally texts of a poetic or fanciful turn that are thus maltreated. Yet a text of a poetic or pictorial turn is such a precious thing in itself that it deserves better of us than this. Why not treat these as they should be treated—textually and poetically at the same time? Let me, as I finish, take one or two subjects which I know have been 'spiritualised'—hideous word!—and see if they can be treated true to their context and true to their poetic feeling.

In Hosea, God promises Isreal, after due repentance, His new favour and restoration: and the prophet sums up His goodness in this memorable line of poetry, 'I will be as the dew unto Israel.' I once heard a sermon by a well-known minister on this text, in which he said, 'First, let us consider the dew as this, (2) Let us consider the dew as that, and (3) Let us consider the dew as something else.' And the truth is, he might have considered the dew as anything he liked, right through the dictionary!

Now, this text is sheer poetry. The only just method of treatment, just to the text and just to the thought, is to take the idea as it lay in the poet's mind. Quite evidently, he compares God's restoring hand to the quickening, enlivening power of the morning dew. Here you have a picture of a hot gasping day in Palestine, when everything droops and wilts under the pitiless heat. But in the gathering twilight, as the air rapidly cools, there falls this gracious dew, which acts like magic on the flagging flowers. By this silent ministry, when the sun rises again in new splendour, the dew-drops glisten like pearls, and the flowers hold up their heads for another brave day.

Why not take the poet's idea, a jewel flashing in the sun, and ask what it is that the dew does for this tired old world? In the first place, you can speak of *the mystery of the dew*, the silent unseen process. Does it rise or fall? When scientists disagree, you can surely be pardoned for calling it a mystery. The analogy between this and the bestowal of spiritual blessing is arresting. There, at some Communion Service, though you cannot explain it, God has whispered to your soul, and in His big, silent ways has given ease and courage to your heart. Passing further, you may show that the dew is *the great restoring power* in times of drought: and in the same way, all blessing, national and spiritual, is for the higher end of strength, for a new day and a new task. If you care, you may pass on to show that the dew is always *strangely proportionate.* In our temperate climate, we have little idea how heavy a dew-fall can be in other, hotter lands. It is only where the heat has been fiercest, that the dew-fall is heaviest. And so, in all God's dealing there is the same law of gracious compensation. 'As thy days so shall thy strength be': as thy need, so shall thy grace be. And finally, keeping to the poet's imagery, you can show that no matter how hot and sultry the day has been, *where there have been clouds*, there is little or no dew-fall, a fact well attested. And so with us, the blessing of God is dependent, not on His willingness, but on our obstructions, the clouds which we put between Him and us, our sins and doubts and obscuring fears.

I commend this treatment of a poetic text because it is not my own. But I mention it as a fair example of how such a subject may be used in line with the poet's idea and true to his feeling. Is there any need to travesty the poet's vision by spiritualising the text?

With diffidence, I shall give you one of my own as a set-off. In Jacob's blessing, the character of Joseph is summed up thus, 'Joseph is a fruitful bough by a well, whose branches run over the wall.' There are two points here, the character of Joseph, and the parable in which he is glorified. The parable is a poetical picture, a vine on the wall, with its roots clustering and matted about an ancient well. Being thus furnished, it grows and prospers finely in the hottest summer. And so rich is its growth that it finally pitches its tumbling branches over the other side of the wall. By the unwritten law of all lands, a weary traveller may rest under its shade by the roadside, and may even pluck some of the ripe grapes which hang alluringly on the roadway. Thus renewed, the tired man goes on his way, comforted by the shade, and refreshed by the fruit of the vine that grew by the well!

Carrying this poetic idea on, you can show how true this was of Joseph, but also how true it is of all good men. If only they have roots about 'the well of God', they prosper. They grow and flourish, and become an unconscious blessing to others. If they have their roots matted round the well, their branches and their fruit are pitched in wild riot over the wall. They do other men eternal service simply by being what they are. The greatest good in the world is the unconscious blessing a good man works by his own goodness. What finer gift can a man give his own age than a good and fruitful life lived in the power of God?

I have finished. However brokenly, I have tried to show you the infinite variety in our subjects and methods, in the hope that by diligence and insight, we may make our ministry as many-sided and as finely toned as possible.

6 The Day of Action

With respect to any final aim or end, the greater part of mankind live at haphazard. They have no certain harbour in view, nor direct their course by any fixed star. But to him that knoweth not the port to which he is bound, no wind can be favourable; neither can he who has not yet determined at what mark he is to shoot, direct his arrow aright.

COLERIDGE, *Aids to Reflection*

In my own day at College, we students had a withering scorn for what we called 'popular preaching'. We thought it good to be coldly intellectual—save the mark!—to reason rather than persuade, and to shun any exaggeration of statement or manner, as if it were an indecency. I remember even the cynical fashion in which we could raise our eyebrows when it was hinted that some man was a 'splasher'.

No doubt this was partly due to a shallow pride and a posturing type of mock intellectualism, summed up in that phrase of Coleridge, quoted in a previous lecture, that 'truth needs not the service of passion'. But as we saw, truth *does* need the service of passion! It generates its own glow. In practice it has driven some of its devotees to astonishing sacrifices. Even cold science—popularly supposed to be so remote and so detached that it has no enthusiasm—has left little mounds of bones at the poles of the world. Grim memorials to *the passion of truth*!

But perhaps our attitude was also due to a righteous and shocked recoil against that type of emotional and catchy preaching which reckons its success by the tears of its audience. This type of sentimental stuff turns many a man from the use of healthy emotion, in a saving fear lest he should exploit the superficial feelings of an audience.

But a sane view should convince us that there is no useful type of preaching, for the ordinary congregation at least, which is not 'popular'. We desire surely to arrest and hold the average worshipper, and be understood by him with ease and assent. Our aim is to touch and move the will, mind, conscience and heart of all our people. We are preaching for divine results, for a verdict for God and the good life. Thus unless we are speaking on particular occasions or on special subjects, preaching must be popular in this fine sense. So long as we are speaking to the people and not to the gallery, for life and not for applause, we need not be ashamed of popular address and popular welcome. I cannot but think that there is often a slight touch of jaundice—or shall I say sour grapes—about our dis-esteem of popular speakers. We so easily affect to despise those qualities that are beyond our own reach, and we believe that it must be something cheap or meretricious that wins success. Remember, it is said of Jesus that *the common people heard Him gladly*.

In what respect can a legitimate study of manner and method, of speech and delivery, be unworthy of a serious-minded man in the Christian ministry? Since preaching is a form of speech, it should be subject to the recognised good laws of effective speaking. Since it is argument and pleading, it should be in conformity with the ordinary rules of thinking and reasoning. And since it is writing and composition, it should observe the rules of good style. Style and form of some sort, both in writing and delivery, are there, whether we will or no. Is there any reason why it should not be the best and most effective style within our range? George Herbert, in describing his ideal preacher, remarks, '*When he preacheth, he procures attention by all possible art.*' Why should he not? Art is good, if it is good art. I am quite sure that there is a call in our work for the development of legitimate graces and gifts, both of method and manner. The subject is well worth our best. To give less is a sneer.

In considering other types of oratory, we observe the toil and passion lavished on their profession by public speakers and actors. There is no study too arduous and no practice too strenuous, if only it leads to mastery: and in their view, perfection is its own sufficient reward. If we contrast this with much of our slovenly and indifferent preaching, it forms a reflection not only on us, but also on our view of the urgency of our message. Indeed, it is an oblique slur on the Gospel.

In any case, it is surely an immense folly to concentrate a week's solid labour and energy on the preparation of a sermon, and give no time at all to its effective delivery. I agree with you that window-dressing by itself is a contemptible thing in the pulpit, manner versus matter. This type of work reminds me of Dean Swift's sketch of the man who wore elaborate lace ruffles to conceal the fact that he possessed no shirt! But on the other hand, as any good business man will assure you, if you have a fine stock of approved material, tasteful window-dressing will do it no harm. Generally, in considering preachers of similar training and ability, I find little difference in the material of their sermons: but there is a great gulf fixed between their methods of treatment and the play of their personality. How often have you heard of speakers with excellent matter, whose effectiveness has been lessened, if not spoiled, by an irritating lack of any art of presentation, or by offensive mannerisms, or by stilted and gawky ways?

To-day, I wish to speak to you about the duty of cultivating your personal gifts, as well as your sermons.

THE DAY OF UNBURDENING

We have come then to the day on which you are ready to deliver the message that you have so studiously considered.

You will not go far before you discover that the first thing that really matters in any service is *atmosphere*. Unfortunately, we ministers have largely to create our own atmosphere. In this we contrast strongly with some types of speakers. The politician usually has an audience that is electric—dry wood ready for the spark. Many of his hearers are as keen, for or against, as the speaker himself. I have been present at political gatherings where the thinnest witticism or the most limping joke was greeted with gargantuan laughter, and a meagre flashy point applauded to the echo. Why? The reason is obvious. The audience is as keen and as thrilled as the speaker himself.

Or take the actor on the stage. People come to the theatre, unless they are blasé, with a sharp expectancy. They bring their atmosphere with them, as one might carry a battery. They are ready to catch up, in a flash, subtle points and hidden meanings. The good actor has at his command an audience self-thrilled and auto-suggested.

Except on special occasions the minister has no such leverage for himself and his message. Sometimes a prominent evangelist or a notable preacher—in an audience more or less prepared or expectant—may count on this gracious atmosphere. That, doubtless, accounts for some part of his impression. But in stated preaching from Sunday to Sunday, you and I cannot reckon on any such helpful forerunner for our work. The people most likely have heard us before. Perhaps they know our ways of thinking and our ordinary methods of treatment. In any case, they are not there expecting great things. The general subject is presumed to be commonly known. Most of all, a large proportion of our people are at church from custom, and without previous preparation behind the 'shut door'. Even when it is not definitely against us, by indifference or a critical spirit, we have to create our own atmosphere, through our use of the Spirit of God in and through our own personality.

I. ATMOSPHERE

In a later lecture I hope to speak to you on the conduct of Public Worship; but meanwhile I refer to this subject to show that we can use the whole service, reverently, for atmosphere—to create a receptive and expectant spirit among the people, so that when we come to our preaching, our sermon may be the natural climax of worship.

I should like to add, on the other hand, that you will be settled in a strange type of church, if you have not some few people who are surrounding you all the time with prayer. You can feel their prayers, as you might smell incense. This is one of the comforts no other type of speaker inherits. In your calling you are quite unique in this. I had an old elder in Forres who once gravely informed me that he had never heard a poor sermon in his life. I know this was not true—I was his minister! But it was true for him in this sense, that he came praying and expecting that God would have something for him, even amid a minister's weakness and folly—an expectation that is never belied. You can count on this then, that amid many disabilities of triteness and lack of keenness, you will have devout souls who are praying you through to victory. Next to God Himself, the comfort of His people is our greatest asset.

The question of atmosphere is of such importance to the

preacher—it means all the difference between receptiveness and dullness—that I shall venture to suggest one or two things for your consideration.

(*a*) Train your people by special teaching in quiet and worshipful ways. Preach an occasional sermon on the theory and purposes of worship. I have found it very helpful, for instance, to speak to the children on the items or parts of the Christian service. (One gain of a children's sermon is that you get home some shrewd hints for the older folk!) I took such topics as these—On the way to church: the first silent prayer: the meaning of the opening voluntary: why do we sing psalms and hymns?: the reading of the word: what is Common Prayer?: the public offering: the sermon: the benediction. You may easily find scope among these things for some useful teaching about worshipful and quiet ways.

(*b*) Instead of scolding people for restlessness or 'coughing'—remember, you *always* lose by displaying irritation!—ask your people occasionally to join with you for a few moments in silent prayer. Prayer in any case is the secret of atmosphere. I know nothing, psychologically and spiritually, that produces a reverent hush like silent prayer. Name some subject round which their prayers should gather—otherwise, many worshippers will only be conscious of an uncomfortable blank! This is not a device or an artifice. In any case, we do not have sufficient congregational opportunities for silent prayer on some timely need.

(*c*) Vary your order. An order is good, but with us it is not a pole to which we are tied. I remember being much impressed by one minister who began his service by saying, 'Let us worship God by hearing His own Word read.' I don't for one moment recommend such a rupture of the usual and approved order. But I mention it to show possibilities.

Do these seem *devices*? I do not mean them to be such. In any case, the surest secret for atmosphere is to have a praying-folk who come with expectation. On our part, it is our duty not to disappoint them.

2. THE NEED OF CONFIDENCE

That leads me to say that you should be strong in all decent confidence. You have many things behind you, precious things. You have your preparation, if it has been honest: your message: your own high purpose: your Christian conviction: your people:

and your God. I said decent confidence. Any confidence that is indecent is—indecent! Nothing makes the average-minded man antipathetic to a preacher like self-assurance.

I believe, however, that a sensible young man suffers more from a prostrating and paralysing fear, arising from a healthy distrust of himself. That often accounts for what is awkward and gauche, and also for what is stilted and unnatural in manner and voice. As young preachers, you have a mingled fear of your audience and yourselves. If you are right-minded, you feel the weight and responsibility of the occasion. Well you may! Yet on the other hand, you have reason for good quiet assurance. Say to yourself something like this, 'I am not here because of myself, or my own cleverness. I believe I have something to say to my people that they ought to know, something that has done good to my own soul, something that the Spirit of God has whispered to me and laid on my heart. And quietly and yet as a herald of God's goodness, I am going now to declare it.' The success of your mission will lie in an assurance of your commission.

3. WHAT IS EARNESTNESS?

This should lead us to the one commanding note in all preaching, *Earnestness*. Earnestness or intensity is not something you put on, as if it were a recognised manner or style of address. There is no good telling a young preacher to be earnest or warm, as if that were a *fashion of speech* he should cultivate. This would only lead to a kind of pietistic insincerity. Earnestness, no matter what form it may take, is the result of one thing and one thing only, the pressure of the message on our own heart, our feeling of urgency, the urgency that marked the disciples. Its best expression is found in the saying attributed to Jesus, 'He who is near Me is near fire.' An earnest spirit is just the glow of an inner flame, kindled and fanned by the special needs of the occasion. For your own soul's sake, beware of affected warmth. Passion is something you feel—it is nothing if it is not *suffering*! That is why I have not much to say to you in these lectures about oratory. I am afraid of oratory in the pulpit, unless it be the natural oratory of a soul on fire. Don't try to be an orator, if you aren't one already! You might as well try to be a poet, without the soul of a poet. Oratory is so easily artificial, a hollow drum, a big manner, with studied effects and sounding declamation. Besides, in any case, I question if oratory of the rounded form is as effective with our generation as it seemed to be with past ages. We are more direct and more simple in these things than our simple forefathers. I believe that an elevated and lively conversational manner is as effective as any style can be. People only smile nowadays at turgid rhetoric; they can't help calling it bombast! Earnestness is a different thing. It may be rhetorical—if rhetoric is natural to the man. But in its essence it is enthusiasm declaring itself, and the deepest note is *conviction*.

We feel that our message is a vital matter for people to know, and that without it, they are in the truest sense lost. Woe to me unless I preach this gospel! This feeling, that he is a bearer of good tidings from God's heart to man's heart, will give any man all the moral passion he needs. It will lead him, for his big purpose, to use himself and his gifts wisely, trained and consecrated, according to their own bent and bias. He may be a candle, a jet of gas, or an arc lamp: but at least he will be lit. With his own endowments—and the greatest sin is to be untrue to them, or to let them lie fallow, or to envy and imitate another man's gifts—with his own peculiar endowments, he will be at his own best high tension, what the Americans aptly call a live wire, a conductor of power. Different men do it in different ways, some by their quietness and some by their vehemence, some by their moments of flash and some by their sustained logic, some by their prose and some by their poetry. That is not the point. Do it in your own way, true to what is characteristic and natural in you. 'Neither will I offer burnt offerings unto the Lord my God of that which doth cost me nothing.'

4. EARNESTNESS AND EMOTION

This suggests a natural corollary. What room should emotion have in our preaching? If we mean by emotion sloppy sentiment, induced pathos, or some tragic manner which we deem appropriate to the occasion—as if we were to scrawl opposite a passage in our sermon, 'Here weep!'—I should answer 'none'. But in the best sense, emotion is a bigger and purer thing than we commonly mean by our use of the term. It is simply the natural reaction of our soul to some big idea or vision: it is our response to truth. There is as fine an emotion of the mind as of the heart—sometimes more moving and generally more lasting.

I believe that emotion has a distinct place in our preaching, provided we give it mingled restraint and dignity, the control of the curb and the rein. The one kind of passion that is effective with an average audience is restrained passion, with emphasis on the restraint. The other type, with a break in the voice and a choked sob in the throat, is only ludicrous. People resent it as a vulgar thing or as a symptom of weakness, and squirm under it with a personal shame. But big ideas have moving power in themselves, for us and for the people, and should touch us as speakers to appropriate moods, which in turn, if they are genuine, will bring their own note into our voice, so that pity, anger or sorrow will find their suitable expression and tone. Emotion may easily be an affectation, but there is a worse affectation for a certain type of 'intellectual' minister—to be casual, to purge the voice of any expressiveness, to leash the emotions like tied dogs, and to empty the tones of the voice until they sound as hollow as a bell.

If we live our words, we shall live their meaning. The elder Dumas, in a famous definition of the essentials of drama, used to assert that all that was needed was 'two trestles, three planks and a passion'—the idea being that the one thing that *did* matter was the passion. A true passion redeems everything, on the stage or in the pulpit. It alone gives creative speech reality and power. All the fripperies, stage-effects and general millinery of the drama will not atone for a false or stilted emotion: but on the other hand, a grand passion will atone for everything. The same is true of the best preaching. Surface emotion, at best a tawdry thing, is particularly nauseating in the pulpit. *But big ideas stir as deeply as high winds, and are as real.* Give your ideas their own emotional value, in your heart and with the people. If passion is sincere and controlled—and remember control gives the impression of reserve power—to suppress it argues a narrow soul.

5. HUMOUR IN PREACHING

I am not so sure about humour, another phase of emotion. Personally, I do not object to a smile in church. Religion need not be a grim business, Carlyle's 'creed of sorrow'. Our Puritan fathers undoubtedly made it too grim. It is true that we are dealing with serious things—God's love, a cross and the tyranny of sin. But our moods are not always serious, nor are our subjects. There is more subtle humour in the Bible than one would imagine—of situation, aspect and retort.

But humour is so dangerous and so readily oversteps all bounds, and further it may so easily wound a sensitive soul—there is nothing that hurts like ridicule—that we may gain by denying ourselves. Certainly where humour is foolishly interpreted as making jokes or witty pleasantries, I should rule it out. One may still quote the prim and lugubrious Cowper,

> 'Tis pitiful
> To court a grin when you should woo a soul:
> To break a jest when pity would inspire
> Pathetic exhortation: and to address
> The skittish fancy with facetious tales
> When sent with God's commission to the heart.

But where humour is rightly understood as a point of view and a way of looking at things, it may be used finely. No gift, however, needs more of the artist, with delicate touch and kindly feeling. At best, very few people are humorous either in or out of the pulpit. So perhaps a wise man had better leave it alone. It is less heinous to be too sedate than too frivolous. Discretion may be the better part of valour.

6. ARMS AND THE MAN

Gesture is *emotion in action*: and its place and function in speaking are as debatable as emotion itself.

Gesture is less important, and more important than most people think. It is less important because it is the one thing that is peculiarly typical of the individual. Nothing is more manneristic than gesture. If it is merely acquired, it may be disastrous. Many people—those who count least—consider it a gauge of liveliness. But unless it is the outcome of a mind and manner naturally lively, it may be annoyingly artificial and stilted. Indeed, most lively speakers would gain by a severe pruning. Some preachers tire us by the absence of any restfulness.

On the other hand, gesture is more important than most people think, for it is the natural outcome of any interested enthusiasm. And as such, when well done, it brings its own power. We need not go the length of Demosthenes who, when asked what was the first quality in speaking, answered 'action', and when asked what was the second quality, answered 'action', and when asked what was the third quality, answered 'action'. But as a natural and trained orator himself, his opinion is worth considering—though I question whether those who addressed the child-age of the world need be an unfailing guide for us who live in a more restrained and sophisticated age.

Our people to-day, with a few exceptions, value restraint. Moreover, they are less influenced by manner than by matter. Action is the first thing which, unless it be naturally beautiful and fitting, annoys by its excess. If one can criticise and control oneself, I should say—keep gesture to its own natural place, i.e. for dramatic or illustrative moments. But do not be afraid to give it its natural place.

Movement, if it is not ungainly or excessive, is good. We are not gramophones, churning out a prepared record: but we are interested men, made lively by living truth, speaking to people who are not above the impression of a good personality. So long as gesture and movement are within the delicate bounds of ordinary refinement, be your own natural self. But beware of extremes: people only smile at a speaker who roams about the pulpit or platform like a caged lion.

Gesture is a kind of *natural emphasis*. It is worth remembering that emphasis *loses* emphasis if it is continuous. In my student days I heard Principal John Caird preaching in the Bute Hall at Glasgow University. For the greater part of the sermon he stood in massive stillness, like a carved statue. Then at the end, he raised both hands slowly above his head, and finished with his hands up, standing silent for a moment. I was never so impressed by any gesture as by that single lonely action. Its peculiar emphasis came from the fact that it stood out like a peak from a level plain.

On the other hand, in the same place, I heard Dr. Matheson, the blind preacher and poet. Perhaps his sad affliction, so heroically borne, made it impossible for him to criticise his own motions, but all through the sermon he had a continuous clutching action with the fingers of one hand, apparently quite unconscious and certainly quite aimless. In the end, such is the power of visible details, I was conscious only of that clutching hand.

Gesture is also a kind of *illustration*. It makes vivid. In dramatic moments it may say more than words, for it goes back to that smothered quality in the human heart, by which in ancient times all emotions were *acted* before they were expressed. We do not wish our preachers to strut like players on the stage: but where emotion is aroused and gesture is the natural outlet of a man's personality, I would rather risk it than see the pulpit impoverished.

We are being brought to-day to an abominable level of trim efficiency. False ideas of propriety are toning down our personal characteristics. We do not have 'characters' any longer in our Scottish villages. They are being crushed out by the dead level of School Board education. It is a loss in national colour. It is a far greater loss in the pulpit. For it is only where there is a true character in the pulpit, with distinctive ways and outlook, that there is real power and appeal. Do not be frightened into being untrue to your own natural gifts. Cut your own wave and be unashamed.

THE SPEAKING VOICE

With some ground for quiet assurance, therefore, and with the natural earnestness typical of your own character and qualities, you now proceed to speak your message. Remember that if God has prepared you, He has also prepared your people.

I. SPEAK TO BE HEARD

The first essential in public speaking is that a man should make himself heard. Not to be heard is fully as bad as not to be understood. They both amount to the same thing, a vacuum. And of course, all nature abhors a vacuum. And after that, there is a vacuum in the pew! Ordinary folk, barring the deaf, have a right to expect that any professional speaker should make himself easily audible. That is why the man is there, *to let his message be heard.*

When people complain that a minister is not heard, I know that the fault may not always be on the speaker's part. There is an alarming number of people who have never trained themselves in the faculty of attention. If people do not attend, the finest voice, like Dr. Johnson's definition of music, is only 'modulated noise'. That however is another matter. Our duty, so far as we can, is to be easily and naturally heard. May I give you a passing hint in this particular? I have had a fair practice now in speaking in many types of buildings. If you know or fear that a church is difficult to speak in, do not begin by loud bawling, as a nervous and inexperienced man is tempted to do. Besides doing no good, that will only tear your throat. Moreover, it is not loudness so much as *good articulation* that makes a speaker heard. Look up to some person in the back gallery, when you announce your first hymn, and see if he catches your words easily and readily. That will give you the measure of the building and the natural pitch of your own voice, and will save you from ineffectual straining.

2. THE NEED OF VOICE TRAINING

This leads me to make a few diffident remarks on the voice. I understand that you have an expert teacher on this subject in your college. May I say that it is folly—a folly which a man will only regret once, and that all the time—if you take this subject of voice-training casually or indifferently. I have met students at college who treated the whole affair with a supercilious disdain—I do not know why—and then they wondered afterwards why their congregation treated them to a dose of the same medicine. Fortunately for myself, I had to face this subject seriously. As a young man, I was afflicted with an abominable stutter. You may thank God if you do not know the exquisite misery and prostration of such a nervous affliction. Then in addition, I had a certain thickness in my speech, the remnant of which still lives with me in my difficulty in tackling the letter 'R'. (What a fine alphabet it would be if that letter were not in it!) Now you have heard about Demosthenes as he walked the sea-shore, with the pebbles rattling against his teeth, in his valiant endeavour to overcome his disabilities of speech. But somehow that does not move us, for Demosthenes sounds far away, and we have deified him into a kind of polite fable. But perhaps it may be helpful to you to see one like yourselves who had quite distinct disabilities to overcome, and who can say that any facility he has in speech is due to honest practice and self-control. If practice and training did that for one circumstanced like me, I hold out hope for any faulty and stuttering speaker. I remember the conduct of an unregenerate schoolfellow when I told him that I was going to become a minister. Like Abraham, he fell on his face and laughed!

I commend to you sincere honest training of your speaking gifts and qualities. In nothing more than in speech does practice induce perfection. Make good use of all sound counsel, and do not be above taking hints from any quarter. To take offence at helpful criticism is a kind of *disguised vanity*.

The aim of a competent master is not to teach you recitation like a parrot, your arms wagging like a semaphore, but to develop your vocal organs that they may have mingled power, modulation and flexibility, and that you may be at ease with yourself. Generally, as you will be told, the secret of audible and likeable speech is that you should attend to your consonants, and your vowels will attend to themselves. The recipe for audibility is not loud or strained talking, but clear enunciation. And you will notice in this matter of articulation that every clear speaker gives his consonants their round value. Aim at ordinary decent cultured speech, natural and unaffected.

Training of the voice may work wonders. Many admit freely that practice along good lines may give power and elasticity to the voice we have. But I claim more than that—it may improve the *quality* of our voice, giving it a depth, a tone and a range that may be an untold gain in our work. If our heart is in our preaching, we shall not think this a trivial matter, or something to be sneered at. I want you to be strong, effective speakers. If you train your mind, you should certainly train the vehicle of its expression.

Do not be afraid of much speaking, if only you talk with ease and an open throat. In mere volume of work, an actor doing, say, a leading part in Shakespeare, or a professor lecturing two hours a day, talks as much in a week as we do commonly in a month: but this never hurts any easy speaker. It will not hurt you, if only you speak naturally and openly.

3. THE TRAGEDY OF THE DRONE

So from that, I pass to say that the only voice to use in the pulpit, in preaching and prayer alike, is your natural voice, used with ordinary modulation and variety. Remember there is no music in a monotone. But there is a sore throat in it for you, and somnolence for your audience! In the offering of prayer there may well be a more quiet and subdued note in speech: but if there is any reverence in our own heart and any appreciation of the occasion, these will of themselves produce all that is needed or appropriate in the matter of dignity or solemnity. There is no such thing as a *dignified style*, except that which is the outcome of natural dignity of mind and mood.

And as for strained talking, pulpit tone, high unnatural pitch or a whining drone, the only thing to be said is that they will annoy an average audience even more than they will hurt you.

I leave to your master in this art to give you wise counsel on many points—speaking on an easy register, maintaining a carrying level, the manipulation of the voice for stress and emphasis, the control of the low note, the use and abuse of gesture, an easy stand, natural unspasmed breathing. Please, don't think you have nothing to learn! Ruin lies that way. In any case, there are few natural speakers in our little world: and even they have countless things to learn. It is fully as hard to be a first-rate speaker as a first-rate singer. When a man makes himself one or the other, behind his apparent ease and at the back of all his natural endowments, there lies *sheer hard work*, with many uncounted victories over the sloth of his own heart.

In particular, be willing to unlearn, and especially to cure yourself of noticeable faults, such as dropping your voice at the end of sentences, and other deficiencies horribly aggravating to a listener. I leave such training confidently to your teacher.

May I add four remarks, however, hoping you will not want to throw brick-bats at me before I finish.

(*a*) *Try to correct your accent, and most of all your pronunciation.* I know you will say it—you haven't got an accent at all! But you have: and so have I. We only notice our accent when we go elsewhere. I remember being amusingly humbled after preaching for Dr. Jowett in New York, when a man said to me that he had not come to hear me preach, but seeing I was advertised as coming from Scotland, he had come to hear my brogue. And here was I, thinking I had no brogue! Let us try to speak as the average good cultured speaker does. We Scots people particularly, if report be true, do not part with anything readily! And we keep our district accents even after the refining processes of university and college. There are more 'accented' speakers in our General Assembly in Scotland than in any other similar body. No doubt you may say the same of yourselves in America.

(*b*) Even more delicately, may I ask you to *beware of some of our localised pronunciations.* I am aware that many hearers are too finical, and rear at an accent more than they would at a misstatement. But I can understand the man who said that he could not listen to a certain preacher, because he was always waiting for two words, 'genuine' with accent on the 'ine', pronounced like 'wine', and 'dirty' as if spelt with a 'u'.

(*c*) Take the opportunity of *hearing as many good speakers and preachers as you can*, and note their methods, both of message and manner. Try to see how they obtain their effects, not for imitation but for guidance. Note their ways and mechanism. See how they handle their subject, and especially how they handle themselves and their own qualities. If you are attached to a congregation, be loyal to it at the morning service; but for you, as coming preachers, I should advocate a little judicious roving. Hear as many men as you can; and while not allowing it to spoil your appreciation, exercise your analysing, observing, and critical gifts.

(*d*) *Speak always according to your subject.* If you have a quiet subject, speak quietly, with ordinary emphasis and stress. If you are preaching on the need of meditation, there is no call to be loud or strident about it. There are some people who think that the only way to preach is to make a noise. 'But the Lord was not in the thunder.' On the other hand, if you are angry, *be angry*. Why shouldn't you be? If you are moved with passion or emotion, be so, naturally and characteristically. It is as much a ministerial affectation to be casual as it is at times to be the reverse. Be as lively in your preaching as you would be in ordinary animated conversation. If you make *that* a test and standard, you will find that it will carry you through. I have chatted with some ministers in my study who have been fascinating talkers—lively, quick and demonstrative—and yet I have been told that in the pulpit they managed to be as wooden as a sawn log! Why should we not be as natural and characteristic in preaching as in conversational discussion? The biggest thing in preaching is lost if we lose our natural vivacity and interest. I think it all comes back to this—be true to your own natural gifts and powers, and use these gifts, trained and sanctified, for the proclamation of your message. Put yourself—nothing less—into your preaching.

TO READ OR NOT TO READ

As a further branch of speaking, I have been asked to give my opinion on the comparative value of the written or the spoken sermon. I think the best judge in every case is the man himself, provided he knows his own powers and limitations. Certainly this is not a subject on which one may prescribe lightly for another, as a doctor would for a patient. Still, it may be worth our while, in closing this lecture, to give the matter some consideration.

British people are almost alone in the world in permitting and valuing read sermons: and in no other profession, even among us, would a read discourse be countenanced. If a member of the House of Commons were to read his speech, it is open to another member to rise and inform the Speaker. 'May I call attention to the fact that the Hon. Member is reading his speech?' And that finishes him! So also at the Bar. Would any advocate, for his own good, dare read his plea, no matter how subtle and intriguing the argument may be? In almost every sphere, except our pulpit, read discourses are not tolerated.

There is no good purpose served in reviewing the historical origin of the read sermon in Britain, except to say that it was originally a device to guard the people against the uneducated preaching of converted priests in the early days of the Reformed Church. But there it is, with us in Great Britain, as an accepted and even welcomed custom. And it is only fair to say that a great body of church people prefer it thus. I wonder if some faint light may not be thrown on this natural preference by an early experience I had in a church at Moniaive near Dumfries, in Scotland. I was a young slip of a student, pleading the 'students' scheme'. As I came into the vestry, the old Beadle asked me if I had my paper. When I replied 'yes', he answered, 'I'm real glad, for a wheen o' thae folk, weel! when they come wi' their paper, ye ken they'll stop when that stops; but when they haven't their paper, the Almichty Himsel' disna ken when they'll stop.' I wonder if it is this 'fear of man'—*the long-winded man*—which is at the root of our national preference for a read sermon. It may be 'without form and void', but at least it has a finish!

I. OUR OPTIONS AS PREACHERS

Generally speaking, there are four styles you may adopt in this matter of read or spoken discourse.

(*a*) You may write out fully, word for word, and read fully, word for word, with of course more or less freedom. But substantially the thing is read.

(*b*) You may write out fully and memorise, repeating or recalling your words as written, reproducing them, as it were, from a photographic plate, or reading off the 'back of your head'.

(*c*) You may write out fully as a discipline in writing, for order, method and language, with the further purpose of clarifying your own mind, and giving your treatment some balance and proportion. Then you may speak it, easily not slavishly, from notes.

(*d*) You may prepare your subject thoroughly, thinking it out as clearly and fully as possible, without putting it down on paper, and then speak your message out of a full mind, trusting to find the appropriate language on your feet.

There is really a fifth possibility—to speak without any preparation at all, extempore thinking as well as speaking, which is the last death, and the curse of a fatal facility.

2. THE NEED OF CONSTANT WRITING

If we take the four serious expedients, there is something to be said for each one of them. But for a young man starting his ministry, whether he reads or preaches freely, writing of some kind is a clear necessity. Writing, in Bacon's phrase, makes an 'exact man', exact in thinking and exact in speech. There is a fine discipline in constant and careful writing which none of us dare sacrifice. Without this drudgery of the pen, we are apt to become loose and sloppy in style. Unconsciously also, we tend to drop into well-beaten grooves both of thought and phrasing, and repeat ourselves. After years of diligent apprenticeship, one may easily lessen the proportion of writing, and may acquire some trained readiness in speech. But until that happy day comes, a wise man will 'play the sedulous ape'.

Joseph Parker of London acquired a unique freedom and power, rich and pungent, in extempore speech. It is reported that a young student, who had admired his sermon, went round to the vestry and asked the Doctor whether he himself should not launch out boldly and try the same method. Parker is reported to have said, 'Young man, I wrote every word I uttered for fifteen years. When you have done what I did then, you can try what I do now.'

3. TO READ OR TO MEMORISE?

(*a*) But apart from writing, which in any case should be unquestioned for the early years of your ministry, should the sermon be read? Well, there is a good deal to be said for the read sermon.

As the old Beadle at Moniaive remarked, it 'stops'. Further, it represents, or should represent, well-weighed and considered material, which is always beside you for further use, unless you are foolish enough to burn it. (Do not burn anything you have ever written—it will keep you humble some day!) But most of all, the written and read sermon, with decent work put into it, has the greater chance of being as full and rounded a statement as a man can give on his topic, well balanced, well divided, and well expressed. There is no reason in the world why it should not be as rich and inspired as the spoken word. I do not see that we may not count on the guidance of the Holy Spirit in the study as well as in the pulpit.

On the other hand, the read discourse can quite easily be cold or lukewarm. To begin with, not many people can visualise their congregation at the desk—enough at least to make the written word direct, intimate, and warm. The sermon may be too detached, too essay-like, and too perfect, 'faultily faultless',

> Chaste as an icicle,
> That's curded by the frost from purest snow.

And further—perhaps most important—it is not everybody who can read. Slavish reading holds a man bound as with chains. Few people ever forget themselves enough, with the manuscript before them. Some people can do 'fell' reading like Chalmers, but they are as rare as Chalmers. I think it needs greater gifts to read well—easily, naturally and powerfully—than to speak well. On the whole, however, in Scotland at least, it is the safe and accepted way. At the beginning especially, amid the quakes of a young minister's early years, it saves a man from fear of himself, his subject, and his people: and it ensures, or should ensure, a balanced and satisfactory treatment of his topic.

(*b*) Of the second method I have nothing good whatever to say. It would murder me to memorise my sermon. As a matter of fact, I couldn't do it, for I don't possess that special type of 'verbal' memory. Any man like me, who can easily stumble in the Lord's Prayer, need never attempt to memorise a sermon! Perhaps in fairness, therefore, I have no right to criticise this method. On the other hand, any time I have heard a minister who memorises, I have received the impression that the sermon is read 'off the back of his head'. There is a subtle suggestion of artificiality in the performance. Very few men who do it are natural and easy. Most of all, it involves a heavy strain on a man's faculties, and in the end, it 'plays the tinker' with a man's nerves. If my advice is worth anything, I should say—read or speak if you like, but do not memorise.

I admit that many notable preachers, especially the group of great preachers who gathered about the court of Louis XIV, memorised their sermons. But on the one hand, they preached only at rare intervals, and more as an oratorical display: and on the other hand, the irrepressible French genius for impassioned declaration and gesture gave life to the dry bones. We unfortunately have to preach often—and we have Anglo-Saxon traditions of moderation and propriety!

4. PREACHING FROM NOTES

The third method is to write fully as a discipline and as a test of balance, and then from notes on a clear scheme, to speak freely. To begin with, this preserves the gain of writing week by week. It ensures that you have worked your subject out in its bearings and due proportion, and that you have defined it, as a piece of thinking, in your own mind in fitting terms. And on the other hand, it assures you freedom and confidence in speaking. You may find, in spite of yourself, that you actually recall sentences as you penned them: but since there is no deliberate and conscious attempt at slavish repetition, this will be no tax or strain on you, and will not limit your freedom. I have known men who have used this method with equal pleasure and effect; and perhaps it is the ideal method of the four. It gives a man's thinking precision and balance. He has his whole subject worked out before him in detail, and suitably paragraphed. He has already, once at least, fitted it into a definite mould of words. And yet he is free in speaking it to alter and adjust as the spirit moves him. All this is at once a happy training in exact writing and definition, and also in free easy speech and delivery, provided—this is always the danger—that he does not try to recall the precise words or phrases coined at his desk.

5. PREACHING OUT OF A FULL MIND

If I had not already said that the ideal method was the third, I should say it was the fourth. At least I shall go the length of saying that after fifteen or twenty years in the ministry, it is the ideal method, for one of the two Sunday services. Perhaps you may reply that from your knowledge of yourself, you know it is not possible for you. But the question is, do you know yourself. I thought I knew myself, until the war came. Up to that time, being as I hinted a nervous person in the pulpit, and believing also that I was verbally bound, I never preached a single sermon that I had not previously written: and in every service, I read literally word for word, though I hope with freedom. I could never have pictured myself preaching from notes: the very thought would have scared me stiff!

Then I was pushed out to speak to a battalion of men, and I knew that the last thing I could do was *read.* So I launched out with a courage only equalled by my timidity. I was so astonished and pleased with my discovery of myself, that when I came back, I resolved that this was too precious a thing to sacrifice. I knew that if I jumped back to the old written and read sermons, I should be a lower man in my own esteem. Somehow, I do not mind other people despising me, but I do not like to have to despise myself.

So purposely, just to keep what I had so narrowly gained, I never wrote out a sermon for the next two years. Instead, I prepared even more carefully than before, and tried to think my subject out in all its details until I could talk it over to the mute volumes in my study, a long-suffering audience. Then I went into the pulpit as full of my subject as I could well be; and with only my points and transitions jotted before me, I trusted to the moment for my language. I missed out a dozen things I should have said. I chased elusive adjectives about like hunted hares. I started sentences and left them hanging in the air like drifting parachutes. I indulged in many impressive pauses. I said things for which I sweated afterwards on a sleepless Sunday night as I recalled the follies of the day. But through it all, as a rock for my slipping feet, was the sublime tolerance of a great congregation.

Now I do not know whether I can advise this for you: but I was desperate to have some mastery of myself. I kept saying to my own soul, 'Be not dismayed at their faces, lest I confound thee before them.' And the moral of this personal apologia, for which I ask your pardon, is—you do not know your own powers, until you have your back to the wall.

Now, mark, you may stand to lose much by this style of preaching. You sacrifice literary touch and grace, neatness of paragraphing, finical exactness, some fine effective phrasing, perhaps balance and poise in your argument—though not so much of the latter as you would imagine, if only you think your points out clearly. You perhaps sacrifice finish and polish and 'built-up' effects. But I wonder if these sacrifices are not more noticeable to you than to your audience? And in any case, I question if they are really sacrifices at all, except to the little golden god of vanity.

On the other hand, there is certainly a great gain by this method in directness and power, in ease and naturalness, in helpful gesture, and the holding power of the eye. I think, too, there is an indefinable link of sympathy and appreciation between an audience and a speaker, when they see that he is thinking along with them. There is more 'staccato' in such speech: but that is a marked gain in speech as in music. A sermon, like music, can be so easy and flowing, with such regular language, that it induces somnolence. Moreover, what you think are awkward pauses and abrupt jagged sentences may be the very element of unconscious power. Mr. Lloyd George, as a speaker, is easily the most effective man I know before an audience. His speeches do not read too well in the next day's papers, but that is not the real test of a speech. You will notice in Mr Lloyd George's speeches the effect of staccato—natural pauses, abrupt sentences, quick changes of method and mood, a speaker's lively interrogations. In most types of popular address, these are strongly effective. Thus, if you feel yourself abrupt and broken, as you certainly will, do not imagine that your audience will necessarily feel it with you.

In these days, especially with men, we stand to gain all along the line if we are direct, simple, straight and pointed in our speaking. I said 'especially with men': for I believe that women have always valued 'form' more than men. That may explain why certain 'nice' speakers have a large female following! But men to-day value direct and robust speaking, and consider *what* you say more than *how* you say it. In any case, by free speech, you will lose less than you imagine, and gain more than you believe. Later on, when you have had some fair experience, take your courage in both hands, prepare your subject thoroughly, and then test yourself in declaring it bravely. You will gain, in any event, by trying every possible method, if you can. Give each a fair extended trial, and choose what suits your own species of genius.

The ideal way—I call it that because it is my own!—is to write and read once, and try one of the other methods at the second service. This will rescue you from the tyranny of one method, and more, from the tyranny of one mood, the detached mood of the desk: it will also give variety to your services. In any case, experiment. If you are trying free speech, such as I have sketched, I should advise a big canvas, a subject or a situation with points and natural developments. The one-idea sermon, at least for the beginner, is too narrow and limiting for free speech. It needs fine handling, delicate transitions and precise phrasing. Generally, it requires a cumulative effect that may only be gained when your subject from beginning to end is all of a piece. But with a subject that has distinct aspects, natural developments, and progress, I do not see why you may not exercise yourself and your gifts in diverse ways.

7 The Theory of Christian Worship

O sweeter than the marriage-feast,
'Tis sweeter far to me,
To walk together to the kirk
With a goodly company!—

To walk together to the kirk,
And all together pray,
While each to the great Father bends,
Old men, and babes, and loving friends,
And youths and maidens gay!

S. T. COLERIDGE, *The Ancient Mariner*

THE CHURCH AS AN ORGANISM

From the earliest times, in friendly homes and elsewhere, Christian people have assembled themselves together for the varied purposes of devotion and work. It would prove or disprove nothing to assert that the Church had never been 'founded', directly or indirectly, by Jesus. For in the very nature of things and by the necessity of its own faith, the Church would have founded itself. *It had to be.* It is an axiom of the Christian situation.

As I see it, the genius of the Christian faith demands that its believers should assemble themselves together, wherever possible. For in the relation of an individual believer to Jesus, there is implied a definite relation of love and service to all other believers and to the needy world. The two hold together, as cause and effect.

As Christians, we are linked together by indissoluble ties, that over-ride all nominal differences. In terms of modern science, we are no longer units, separate and self-contained, but we 'fly together' and cohere, as the atoms of a new and more wonderful creation—a spiritual world within the physical.

On the one hand, Christians must assemble themselves together *for their own good*, since fellowship is inherent in the Christian idea, and blessing comes from fellowship; and on the other hand, *for the good of others*, since the implications of our faith are bindingly aggressive and missionary. In a true sense, an isolated or separatistic Christian is a contradiction in terms. For his own growth in grace, a true disciple dare not cut himself adrift from the inspiration and blessing of common worship. He has something unique to receive from this, and something equally unique to give. Without this mutual giving and receiving, his own spiritual life is impoverished both in content and quality. Still further, he dare not sever himself from the prayers and active co-operation of his fellow-believers if he ever hopes to aid or fulfil the dream of his own faith, begotten within him by Jesus, *the coming of the kingdom of God among men.*

Thus the idea of the Church as an aggressive co-operation of believers, and even as an *institution*—an organised unity apart from and bigger than the mere collection of individual Christians—is already forecast by the logic of the situation and the logic of our own personal faith in Jesus. In other words, the Church with its common worship and common action is a necessary result of Christian belief. I do not think it is worth arguing whether Jesus ever contemplated the founding of such a visible organisation. It is sufficient that the Spirit of God, in the hearts of believers, *compelled it to be.*

WHAT IS WORSHIP?

Worship is the Church on its knees. The derivation of the English word may give us a suggestion of its deepest meaning. Worship is simply the ascribing of 'worth' to God. We are aware of all His gifts, around us and most of all in Jesus: and we meet in high gratitude, reverently and joyfully, to praise His name. Thus worship is transcendent wonder—wonder at the Divine nature and work in providence and grace—wonder that bursts into praise, as naturally as the unfolding of a flower.

Christian worship is God, seen and adored through the life and cross of Jesus, who is the supreme proof of God's goodness. If God is the object of all worship, Jesus is its channel. We worship God for and in Him. He is our living way, by whom we know and praise the Father for the majesty of His goodness and love.

As a personal act, Christian worship is a soul relating itself to God in Jesus Christ—seeking communion, offering praise as a sacrifice, receiving grace and blessing. It is a *fellowship of spirits*, the human with the divine. We meet in our Christian service for two ends, to give and to receive—to give praise and adoring thanks, to receive pardon, direction and peace from God, and the benefits of communion with our fellow-believers. In one sense, as individuals, we are alone with God, because all religion in the last resort lies in the personal relation of a soul to its Maker. In another sense, we as individuals are lost and swallowed up in the congregation, for there are clear gains of fellowship, corporate blessing, that dare not be sacrificed. The rewards of worship are like 'the dew unto Israel', mysterious but real.

As fitting as many other inadequate descriptions, man might be defined as 'the animal that worships'. He has a sense for the infinite that drives him to his knees in fear or in love. He is aware of the unexplained and perhaps the unexplainable: he knows that above him there is some 'power not ourselves that makes for righteousness'. And in one sense, the glory and tragedy of history is man's groping after God if haply he might find Him.

But natural worship does not explain Christian worship. Here the call is more definite. We may summarise this call in these few points: (*a*) Fellowship with believers is inherent in our faith. (*b*) Christ's own practice is our model. He attended the prescribed worship of His own day—'as His custom was', says St. Luke—and He called the disciples apart for corporate prayer and communion. (*c*) The example of the Apostles is binding—and especially their recommendation that we forsake not the assembling of ourselves together. (*d*) Jesus has promised that where two or three are gathered together in His name, He will be specially present, an assurance of particular grace in fellowship. (*e*) There are undoubted spiritual gains in Christian intercourse—of sympathy, help and inspiration. (*f*) Christ's dream of a regenerated world is only possible as Christians act together in some form of massed unity.

WORSHIP IN THE EARLY DAYS

In the nature of things, the meetings of the early Christians for worship and work were remarkably simple: and during the first century and part of the second, they remained thus free and simple. The reasons for this are not far to seek. To begin with, Jesus their Master had left His people no rules or rites—unless we except the Lord's Supper. He bequeathed to them only the dynamic of His message and person, leaving future developments to the control of God's Spirit and to the wisdom and spiritual insight of His people.

At the outset, bereaved so unexpectedly, the disciples met frequently for their own comfort: and for these gatherings, then and later, they devised simple ways of administration. At first, they naturally followed their ancient and honoured model, the formal worship of the synagogue. But they soon discovered that the new wine burst the old bottles. The flood of God could not be confined to a canal. Hence, the first note of Christian development was *a break with ancient formalism*, not because the disciples objected to forms, but because the forms themselves were hopelessly inadequate. The astonishing joy, the rapture, the intoxication of their new faith could not be compressed within ancient rituals. As well seek to bottle up the blue ocean behind stone dykes!

Thus, for the early Christians in their new elation, worship was free and unconfined. Quite evidently at first they adopted the ideas and customs of *private devotion* in their corporate worship, with the liberty of the individual unchecked, retaining even the speech and methods of private individual prayer. Thus, common prayer was simply private prayer enlarged in scope and range, and spoken aloud. But growing experience, reflection on the purposes of devotion, and also the natural psychology of an audience inevitably made corporate worship less individual, less free, more arranged, more comprehensive, and even more formal. Within a short time we learn that the Apostles were forced to counsel order and decency, as against the unrestricted freedom of leaderless worship.

In the book of Acts and in other early records, we can readily picture the extreme simplicity and naturalness of these Christian gatherings. The disciples and converts met in houses, large rooms and halls, where such were available: and they exhorted and inspired each other in the faith, seeking mystical union with their Lord by simple ways of remembrance and devotion. Naturally, there were no officials or leaders as we understand the term, until in time, for the ends of decency and order, suitable men were chosen for the regulation of worship and the work of evangelisation.

If we take the records of the first century, we can easily picture the items of these services—if we except, of course, the root of most Christian or un-Christian controversy, the Lord's Supper. Examining these records, we find the following parts of early worship fairly well defined: (*a*) *Praise* in simple unrhymed psalms or hymns, many of which are preserved for us in the text of the New Testament, like fossils embedded in rock. (*b*) *Prayer* in free and spontaneous utterance. (*c*) *Testimony*, the personal witness of people who had been touched by God's Spirit. (*d*) *Reading of the Word*, at first the Old Testament, and later, the messages and records of the Apostles, and the Discourses of Jesus. (*e*) *Preaching and teaching*, for the guidance of believers and for the conversion of the pagan world.

Even the Lord's Supper, round which the debates and acrimonies of the ages have so unseemly gathered, was unquestionably celebrated at first in the simplest manner. In its actual setting, this supper was the conclusion and crown of a common meal—as with Jesus and the Apostles at the Passover—where the disciples were gathered in fellowship, and where, as the meal finished, they used the materials on the table for a sacred symbol of the sacrifice of Jesus. They offered up a fervent prayer of thanksgiving—their 'sacrifice'—and then in silence they partook of the bread and wine in remembrance of their Lord and as a token and seal of their mystical union with Him.

THE RIGHT TO DEVELOP

Now, I do not say that the Church should be tied to these ancient simple forms, which were largely the outcome of the special circumstances of the day. To do so would be as foolish as it would be disabling for the modern Church. Surely the Holy Spirit did not cease to function in the hearts of believers at Pentecost! But at least it may be said that these simple methods of worship were the free choice of those who best knew the simplicity of Jesus and understood His aversion from Pharisaic forms and ritual. However we may have departed from them in our day, we must frankly admit that they agree with the mind of Jesus, as we have it revealed throughout the Gospels. They certainly express worship in spirit and in truth: they are natural, unadorned, simple and sincere, like the Man of Galilee Himself. Those friends who knew

Jesus in the flesh and who were as yet uninfluenced by heathen views of splendour or grandeur considered these simple services sufficient for them and in line with their memories of our Lord, whose personal approach to God was so direct and immediate.

All this may be an argument for the retention of such simple forms of worship, in unadorned naturalness. But on the other hand, we claim, and rightly, the liberty to develop. To be hidebound to forms, however simple and bare, is in itself a formalism. As the 'Epistle of the Society of Friends' remarks, 'pure worship under the Gospel stands neither in forms nor in the formal disuse of forms'. Liberty and freedom in worship would be as much ruined by the dominance of *simple forms* as by elaborate ceremonial. It is only a difference of degree! A man may be as much a prisoner in a den as in a palace. The only true liberty is the liberty to move and grow and develop, the liberty if need be to *change*. Hence, the Church, in every age, has rightly claimed this privilege of growth and progress.

I. THE SILENCE OF JESUS

The question appeals to me in two aspects. On the one hand, since Jesus prescribed no definite rules and ordinances, excepting perhaps the Lord's Supper, to govern the practice of His people, we may affirm that it lies in the wisdom of the developing Church to adjust itself and its ways to the changing needs of the generations, and to devise helpful rites and symbols for the good ends of devotion. One openly admits this right of development, claimed and used by all churches in greater or less degree. We believe in the directing and suggesting wisdom of the Holy Spirit, who has promised to lead us into all truth. Whatever happens, we must hold to that.

But on the other hand, I find myself ready to admit that the fact of Christ prescribing no rules for His worshipping people may be used, finely and powerfully, as an argument for unadorned and simple worship, free from limiting forms, such direct and immediate worship as undoubtedly characterised the Church of the Apostolic days. These people were nearer to Jesus, and knew His free and informal outlook. The determining thing in Christian worship is not what pleases us, not even what *helps* us, but what is most true to our Lord's practice, His habit of mind, and His own direct approach to God.

I know that some people will reply that many of our modern developments in method and ritual *aid their devotion.* At first sight, that seems a fair answer. But in some ways, religious aids, especially if derived from other religious sources, may be the subtle enemy of Christianity. These religious aids, so common in natural religion and largely derived from it, may be extremely helpful for those who are groping in the dark, as a crutch helps a lame man. But Christians who have seen God's heart in Jesus are not in the dark. Their communion with Him is sure and immediate. Regarding many of the practices and rituals of modern churches, the question is not, '*do they aid devotion*?' but '*are they Christian*?' Our test is, and can only be, the mind of Jesus. And I am convinced that the surer a man is of Jesus as God's pure revelation, the less will he tend to rely on these broken lights. Natural religion needs all the aids it can discover, for anything that brings the dim God nearer is good for it. *But what helps natural religion may ruin Christianity!* I repeat that the decisive question regarding all aids to devotion is not 'are they helpful?' but 'are they Christian, as we know Jesus in the New Testament?'

However we settle it, I feel sure of one thing—we are on the horns of a dilemma. Either the Church may seek to model its present services on the simple pattern of those early days, keeping spirituality, freedom and simplicity in the forefront, or it may frankly claim the right to develop with changing days and needs. But we cannot have it both ways, as some of us would like. If we claim the right to advance and change, can we also claim, as some churches so confidently do, that our practices are either ancient or original? I feel inclined to remind you of the homely proverb, 'You cannot eat your cake and have it.' Claim the right to develop and change, if you wish, but do not also assert that your developed rites and forms are ancient and original.

2. THE GROWTH OF SYMBOLS AND RITES

After the second century, development rapidly overtook the common worship of Christian people. Not only were the early freedom and simplicity gradually replaced by prescribed liturgies and fixed ceremonial, but even the theory of worship became gravely altered. As the 'leader' developed into the 'priest', the service and the sacraments became sacerdotal in character, until the ancient simplicities of early faith were swamped beyond memory. Without any doubt, much of this change, in form and idea, was due to the subtle but sure invasion of pagan notions of 'splendour' as regards method and significance. The new converts, among all types of peoples, had been accustomed naturally to imposing ceremonials in their own faith: and ritual seemed a necessary part of *any* faith. The Church, with fine intention and no doubt with a fine dream for Christ, entered on a slow process of *accommodation*. It appropriated the Feast Days of the popular religions and gave them a Christian significance, or at least a Christian name. Many of the ideas and theories of the mystery religions of the age were taken over and 'Christianised'. Where whole nations or blocks of people were converted in a day, as by royal order, what else could be done, if the untrained converts were to be held? This kindly accommodation perhaps saved the world of that day for nominal Christianity—but accommodation is always bought at a price. The exact price was this—that in trying to swallow the world, the Church was swallowed by the world. It is difficult for me—I honestly admit my covenanting heritage!—to find much of the lowly Jesus of Galilee or the justifying faith of the Apostles in the imposing grandeur, the hierarchical ranks, or the magic ideas of the modern Church. It is reported that Julian, the defender of paganism, exclaimed as he died, 'Thou hast conquered, O Galilean!' But it might be as subtly true to say, 'Thou hast conquered, O Julian!'

I am not stating this as a *charge*—for I have admitted fully the right to develop—but I am stating it merely as a historical fact. Whether it was a good or foolish change is not in question. The point is, there was *change*—and so radical a change that the new worship differed from the old not only in degree but in kind.

With the Reformation came a desire to reverse the whole process, and to discard anything and everything that could not be justified from the New Testament. Without doubt, this was a narrow stand to assume—a full-grown Church perched on the stool of an infant society! The Reformers' zeal—so dangerous because it was really a *zeal*—ended by cutting the ground from its own feet. The men of the Reformation did not halt to ask any of the wise questions we might have asked. They did not enquire whether symbolism is an aid to worship, and only the *excess* of it is dangerous. They did not wonder whether lame human souls might not find 'ritual' a useful crutch in their search for God.

They hardly stayed to speculate on the aids of art for true devotion. They were only filled—and I can understand them—with a passion to clear away the rubbish-heap of superstition and paganism that had hidden the jewel of God from the eyes of simple seekers. Thus, according to our view, to which we are entitled, the Reformers were either foolishly thorough or thoroughly foolish.

The aim of the Reformation, then, was to effect a return to the simple trusting faith and the natural unadorned worship of the Apostolic age. Whether this is either possible or desirable for us to-day is another question. Luther and his band hammered and hewed, until the encrustations were chipped from the walls, and the stones were laid bare. The modern query is—*are they too bare?*

DIFFERENT PATTERNS OF WORSHIP

I. THE TWO EXTREMES

From this short sketch we can now see that there are two opposing ideals of a Christian service in modern practice. Amid many shadings and approximations, there are these two contrasted types:

(*a*) At the one end, we have a simple free and unornate worship, where extreme naturalness and elasticity are the main notes, and where no fixed order is either prescribed or compulsory. This does not imply the absence of order, but only that there is no compulsion other perhaps than custom and usage and the requirements of decency.

(*b*) At the other end, we have an elaborated, fixed, formal and generally ornate service, where prescribed forms and liturgical fashions are predominant. This does not necessarily imply that there is no liberty but only that the area of freedom has been strictly settled and defined, the poles between which the service may freely swing.

In the one service the people *deliver themselves over* to the individual leader, trusting to his fitness and preparation: in the other, the people *deliver themselves from* the individual leader, especially from his moods, eccentricities and angularities. I admit of course that there are many gradings between these two forms of worship. Indeed, there are many types that partake of both. But for my purpose now, I may assume that this clear contrast holds good.

Now for those people who are not hide-bound and who do not prejudge the case by their own inclinations or their own inheritance, the problem in church worship to-day is the relation of these two types of service to each other. In their extremes we must admit that they are frankly opposite—like oil and water, they do not mix. Indeed, I question whether 'mixing' might not ruin both, spoiling the unique beauty of each and retaining only their common dross. It is also fair to admit that there are types of Christians—so wide and generous is Christ's net—who will only be satisfied or helped by one or the other. It is a very narrow-souled man who speaks of a 'right' or a 'wrong' type of worship. Ideally, what suits each soul and each age best, bringing God near, is best for it. In no place is dogmatism more hurtful than in the sphere of preferences.

I have one good friend who could not worship as I do: and if I worshipped with him I should be starved. I may prefer one type of service for myself—as I certainly do—but surely I need not dogmatise for anybody else. My duty is to interpret the mind of Jesus, as He speaks to me in the New Testament, and to be loyal to my own vision of the truth. But it is a joy for me to know that others can worship Him in other ways, perhaps to them larger ways. It is no little part of the genius of Jesus—speaking of Him as a religious teacher—that He allowed this gracious latitude. He sent the healed lepers back to their appropriate worship. He himself could praise God in the Synagogue or the Temple, on the Mount of Olives or by the lakeside. Faith and love were primary: methods were secondary. Why need this diversity of worship worry us? To my mind, the very difference and complexity of Christian varieties is a gain, a gain both in richness and in colour. I should be the last to wish that either individuals or churches should be brought to a common level. A common level is so often a dead level. The question of unity, so loosely talked of to-day, seldom troubles me, at least so far as uniformity of worship is concerned. So long as men and women are different in build and outlook, they must be allowed to think differently, and of course worship differently. The prevalent divisions in party politics seldom alarm us. Rather, we urge that these divisions argue health and vigour of mind, a moving and thinking people. Only when men cease to care passionately for their own vision of truth, do they readily sacrifice their differences. But a union on these terms would not be a unity but a laxity. Even if a comprehensive union were to be realised, I should still hope that there would be room, as there would be need, for diversities of worship. In any event a union that meant mere *uniformity* would be a disaster, if it were not first an impossibility! Meanwhile, amid different ideals of worship, let us exercise the grace of charity and admit freely that those who differ from us are at least as sincere as we are, and are emphasising a needed complementary truth, without which the Christian circle is incomplete.

2. CAN THE TWO IDEALS BE MERGED?

Still for many thoughtful people the relation and possible rapprochement between these two types of worship is a question of the moment. Can the fixed service become more free and less formal, and the free service more fixed and less individual? Can liturgical worship grow more untrammelled without serious loss, or free worship more liturgical without sacrificing spontaneity? I have some friends in the Church of England who would welcome the one: and there are many in my own Church who would be grateful for the other. One or two fellow chaplains of the Episcopal Church informed me that on occasion they frankly scrapped the prescribed liturgical service with their men in France: and on the other hand, many of us know that a modified liturgical order might rescue our worship, and our people, from the gaucherie, the blatancy, and indeed the irreverance of some of our moods and our ministers.

Many of the 'free' churches, and especially Presbyterian churches overseas, have travelled so far that they have compiled an order of service which amounts to an optional liturgy. (Part of the freedom of a Free Church, remember, is that it may bind itself with an order and a liturgy, if it so wishes. The whole range of devotional literature and the diverse methods of all churches are open to its choice. A Free Church is the true eclectic). The Methodist Church in England, unless I err, has had this fine privilege of an optional liturgy in its hands for years. What use is made of it, and what gain may come from it, I do not know. But on our own side, what I do know is this—that many of our 'free' ministers use an unconscious liturgy of their own, Sunday by Sunday, grooves of thought and expression as stereotyped as any printed thing, with this important difference, that their unconscious liturgy is often gravely ill-balanced, crudely expressed, cruelly omissive and without any of the dignity, comprehensiveness and haunting beauty of the ancient prayers of the Church.

I predict that you as young ministers may have to consider this question in all its bearings within your own generation; and perhaps you may find many of the people as ready for some *via media* as you may be yourselves.

THE CONDUCT OF A 'FREE SERVICE'

Meanwhile I am asked to speak to you on the conduct of a 'free service', such as is common in our Protestant churches.

Generally, this type of service delights in the ancient simplicities of Christian worship. These simplicities, it may be said, need not be either bare or barren, but may have a magnificence and stateliness native to themselves. In any adequate sense, the *grandeur* of worship does not depend on external or adventitious aids—symbols, robes, music or processions—though with some minds these may be eminently helpful and impressive. But grandeur consists always and only in *spiritual qualities and effects*—the ordered praise of a worshipping people, the controlling ideas that master their hearts, and the sense of the real presence of Jesus among His disciples, what I might call the 'march of God' through the service. Fortunately this is quite independent of differing methods and practices of worship, and may be equally present in all. There may be as much grandeur in the meeting of a thousand men on a hillside, chanting a covenanting psalm, as in the most ornate service of a high cathedral. Grandeur is never in the *method* but in the *spirit.*

On our part, we hold to these simple forms because we believe that they are least unlike the simplicity of Christ's worship and Christ's personal approach to God, and also because they are in accordance with the early spiritual worship of the young Church.

On the other hand, while we realise the value of symbols and rites, we realise also their danger. In process of time, all symbols tend to outlive the aspirations and ideas that first gave them birth, and may end in becoming valued for their own sake. A religion that is rich in ritual needs a more constant and studied return to the sources of inspiration than any other, lest the people should accept the symbols for their own value and forget the ideas they shadow forth. This is no fancied danger, as history so eloquently proves. The fault may not lie in the use of symbols, as symbols: but it certainly lies with those who use the symbols—with the old, sluggish, complacent human soul! Remember, however, there may be just as much unspirituality in the barest and baldest service. Absence of form may not save any one of us from formalism.

Our question to-day is, how shall we make our free service as rich and satisfying as possible? For this purpose, I think it is expedient to have quite clearly before us, now and in each particular service, *our objects as worshipping Christians.* What do we come to a service to express, be it in word or symbol?

For what it is worth, I might sketch to you my ideal of a free service. I prefer rather to speak of governing principles, knowing that nothing settles details like theory—and without a saving theory, the most perfect details are a formalism. My ideal service (is there such a thing, for I find my ideal changes as growth does?) might be of little help to you or your people. And perhaps vice versa? I believe that what we need to know, above everything, is the theory of worship—its aims, principles and qualities. If we have some grasp of these, *they* will determine the rest for each of us in our own circumstances.

THE PURPOSE AND THEORY OF WORSHIP

I. AN EXPRESSION OF GRATITUDE

The first and greatest note in any service is the *expression of gratitude.* Public worship is the recognised means for exhibiting the gratitude of Christ's people for the known mercies of God. I believe firmly that this expression of thanks should take a foremost, even dominant, place in all Christian services, and generous room should be allowed for it in praise and in prayer. If we realise in any adequate sense our burden of indebtedness week by week, this will impart an adoration, a dignity, and a wonder to our worship that will be uplifting and cleansing. Avoid any familiar note in your worship that might imperil this constant sense of wonder and gratitude. Among the traditional sayings of Jesus, I value greatly that one quoted by Clement of Alexandria, 'He that wonders shall reign: and he that reigns shall rest. Look with wonder at that which is before you.' I know of nothing that cheapens life and worship alike—and worship, whether formal or free—so much as the idea that things are to be taken for granted. To take nature for granted: the daily miracle of life for granted: the providence of God for granted: even the cross of Jesus for granted—that empties worship of any saving grace.

If is worth noting, as history will show you, that worship of any kind or form has always degenerated as soon as this controlling astonishment has been lost. Our Scottish Calvinism may have been a hard, unbending, even logically cruel thing: but what gave the Calvinistic church its unfailing, dignity and power was its prostrating sense of awe—wonder at the decrees and sovereignty of God, and wonder at His unmerited mercy. And this produced a dignity of Christian life and worship that has marked all Calvinistic creeds. But the secret here and elsewhere is amazed gratitude.

This renascence of wonder in worship will save you from some of the failings which we deplore in certain spheres. On the one hand, it will save you from cheap *familiarity* in language and methods. It will prevent you from talking to God in the light and casual terms in which you address your next door neighbour. And on the other hand, it will rescue you from the slack and sloppy *sentimentalism* that ruins true reverence. Avoid speaking about Jesus as 'dear Jesus', 'lovely Lord', 'sweet Saviour'—terms which, to say the least of them, are utterly alien to the robust thought of the New Testament. No one wants starched dignity: but we do want reverence.

May I suggest that you speak to your people occasionally about the ideals and theory of worship? Your congregation in its knowledge or ignorance may deepen or ruin your atmosphere. Call on your people to come into God's presence with humble and adoring minds: ask them to gaze with amazed eyes at Jesus: show them a daily cause for astonished gratitude at the cross of the Lord. If this sense of wonder is not present, all the elaborate rituals will not impart grandeur: if it is present, the singing of a plain psalm may be a new revelation of grace! I cannot see how worship can possess any dignity or exalting greatness, if God's glory and Christ's sacrifice are thought of as trivial or accepted things. Educate your people in this faculty for wonder.

Above all things, train your people to bow their heads in prayer as they assemble in church. I believe the key of the service—and the secret of atmosphere—is not in the prayer of the preacher but in the opening silent prayer of the worshipper. Instruct your young people especially on this matter, and suggest to them the thoughts and petitions which should be in their hearts. This silent prayer tunes the worshipper to great things: it gives him the spirit of expectancy. But best of all, it tunes him to sympathy with the service and the preacher. It takes away the critical and biased spirit, and puts him in gracious concord with the worship and the worshippers.

2. TO MEET WITH CHRIST

We come to Christ's church *to meet Christ Himself*, actually and really. Thus, the next secret of the service is to believe in the 'Real Presence'. The Roman Catholic Church effects this through its magical symbols: and this belief in the Real Presence is one of the sources of that church's amazing power. But a Real Presence in bodily form, such as is obviously inferred in the Mass, is a poor thing compared with *the spiritual presence of the risen Lord.* Tell people quite frankly that they may meet God anywhere: but tell them as frankly that they meet Him in a unique sense among the assembly of Christians. The Lord is there! Gloriously there!

Now, if we ministers believe this—and our people too—reflect for a moment on the difference such a belief will make in worship. It would impart life and fervency to the whole service, to us in our conduct and leadership, and to the congregation in its expectancy. We come, as I said, to express gratitude to God: but more than that, we come to meet Jesus, to meet Him who is the source of our greatest gratitude. Keep this in your minds in planning your service. On our part there will be no lack of preparation for the items of worship if we remember it.

3. TO EXPRESS OUR COMMON NEED

We come to express *our great common need*, and to receive God's promised grace. Under this, we should have three things clearly in mind.

(*a*) The confession of sin and the request for pardon. The biggest passion I know in a good man's life is his longing for the cleansed life. Quietly, openly and faithfully, without hypocrisy and without reservation, with no excuse or condoning qualification, we confess sin. In Christ's name, we expect the pity and pardon of God. It will exalt our worship if, here, most of all, we see the wonder of God's nature—that for no claim of ours but just for the inconceivable love of His own heart, we are received as His sons. On the other hand, in your teaching about the service, have no unworthy views about God or about forgiveness. Reveal God unmistakably as King as well as Father, in the majesty of His righteousness as well as His gracious pity. And tell your people frankly that even omnipotent God cannot forgive the heart that will not repent.

(*b*) In the service of common worship we seek direction and help amid the moral puzzles of daily life. We live amid tangled motives: problems confront us each day: duties are difficult and teasing: our pathways branch and leave us in moral questioning. The Christian service under your guiding—in all its details, prayer as well as preaching—should meet this deep need. Many worshippers are present looking for a pointing finger. Let the whole service reveal the message of Jesus for troubled souls, showing them Christ's plain way, and assuring them that no man was ever lost on a straight road.

(*c*) The service, by its moral quality, should vitalise the will, and lead the worshippers to the spirit of obedience. Worship that has not this strong quality is valueless. It may be sensuously beautiful and deeply emotional: but worship is more than praise, it is *life*. Every service is a failure that does not strengthen the spirit of obedience and moral resolve.

I am tempted to warn you here against *emotionalism* in the items of your worship. There are some types of service—formal and informal alike, evangelistic as well as ritualistic—that affect us like an intoxication, but the emotion aroused also passes off like intoxication, quickly, and leaving us with a lowered tone. Now there is an actual spiritual *loss* in being moved if our emotion is not translated into life or action. An emotion that does not cleanse, or does not affect character and conduct, is worse than useless—it is a moral danger! For we emerge from it as from a drug or anæsthetic, with a kind of relief, as if from an unhealthy state: and it leaves us not the same as before, but worse. For—here is the point that we as ministers should remember—every emotion that has been *felt and rejected* leaves the worshipper a lower man. Keep your services free from shoddy emotional effects—and much of our modern music deserves the charge—for in the end, these things only harden a man's soul.

4. WE MEET FOR FELLOWSHIP

I have spoken of this already in passing, and it is so evident in itself that I shall not stay to emphasise it. Except this—if there is a fellowship of worship, there is also a fellowship of action. The worship of God is not an end in itself—either here or in heaven—unless it leads to the finer worship of a pure life and concerted action for the world's good. The Church worshipping should be the Church working. It is on its knees that it may rise to its feet. Keep before yourself and your people the fact that worship is only perfected in work.

So far we have spoken of the theory and the purposes of our common worship. With these in our mind, leavening our thoughts, we may now discuss some qualities which should pervade our service, and the means by which these qualities are made possible.

THE QUALITIES OF CHRISTIAN WORSHIP

I. THE NOTE OF JOY

I put foremost the *note of joy*. This is the peculiar gift—above laughter, gaiety or even happiness, for it can be present when these are absent—this is the peculiar gift Jesus bequeathed to the world. It should be in every Christian service, even a funeral service—most of all there, for Christ has conquered death! Generally, our worship is too mournful and plaintive: our music is too sad and 'minor': our prayers and prelections are too lugubrious: and as a rule we speak and think too much about sin, and too little about grace. It is a serious misreading of the genius of Christianity that could make a man like Carlyle define our religion as the 'creed of sorrow'. If it is anything at all, it is the creed of victory, a dream of redeemed manhood in a redeemed world. But we ourselves are to blame. We have focused our thoughts on the 'stations of the cross' instead of the stations of glory! We come to worship with sober clothes and sober faces, and we wrap ourselves in a ponderous silence that chills every natural emotion. We confuse reverence with solemnity, and serenity with propriety. What a solemn, dull business an average service is! Little wonder that young people misconstrue religion as something that *robs* human life instead of enriching it!

Now, the first thing that pagan critics noticed in the disciples was that they possessed something positive and electrifying which they themselves lacked, a sheer joy that played over them like magic. And further, the first thing any unbiased observer to-day notices in Jesus Himself is His contagious serenity, a trustful and happy peace that no misfortune seemed able to disturb. Why is this so noticeably absent from our services? I believe our best embassy for religion is our note of joy. We have deep reason for joy—we are forgiven, we are held and saved amid temptation, we can face to-morrow in the assurance of God. The early Apostles impressed the world by this note of supremacy, in the strength of a Christ not dead but living. I do not suggest that there should be anything loud or unrestrained in our worship. The Apostles had to govern that garish type of joy in the early Church, the joy that bursts bounds and defeats itself by reaction. But the deepest joy is one that is serene and confident, like the quiet and ordered sunshine of a summer's day. Sometimes, joy is so big that it sobers! Yet frankly, in spite of historic misdemeanours, I would rather risk the joy that breaks bounds like a rising flood than interpret our religion as a thing that is only decent and proper and unthrilled.

Some means to this end are quite obvious. Choose triumphant praise, and dwell on thanksgiving in your prayers. I do not suggest that you overlook or forget need and suffering—they are more present than any of us can ever know—but I ask you to look through them and see the dawn. For your own preparation of soul, before you enter the place of worship, read two types of passage: (1) something like the thirty-second psalm, 'I acknowledge my sin unto Thee, and mine iniquity have I not hid', and (2) something like this, 'Who shall separate us from the love of Christ? Nay in all these things we are more then conquerors through Him that loved us.'

To express the joy and hope of the Christian soul and also the dream that should master our hearts, may I suggest a symbol for your Communion Table? (Do not ban all symbols as unspiritual: they may be of great spiritual profit, if rightly used, if the symbols suggest not themselves but the ideas they embody.) My strange symbol is this. Instead of the mop-headed chrysanthemums and the sickly white lilies with which it is common to adorn the Altar or Communion Table—few people, I imagine, ever reflect *why* they are placed there, except that they look 'nice'—put rather, some Sabbath morning, a little globe of the world. Like the communion itself, that would be a silent sermon! Even to the child's heart, it would whisper the needs of the world for which Christ died and of which the Altar itself is a symbol. And most of all, it would reprove all self-complacent worshippers and save the Church from being a polite social club. The worshipping church, if its own worship is to be worthy, must have its eyes set on the redemption of the world. For us to see only the Church and miss the kingdom of God is a tragedy.

2. WORSHIP IN THE SPIRIT

The second quality of good worship is *spirituality*, a word expressing something we can easily recognise or miss, but cannot as easily define. Christ desired our worship to be 'in spirit and in truth'. God is a spirit, and spiritual worship is the communing of our soul with His, our commerce with God. That may be done with or without forms or symbols, the one equally with the other. We people of the free churches too easily assume that spirituality means an absence of artificial aids: but the truth is, some people worship more spiritually with forms than without. The secret is to have commerce or transactions with God, however it is done, by sincere faith appropriating His offered mercies. If forms and rituals help some souls, then God bless forms! Personally, I can worship best in simple ways of praise and prayer, and need no mediatory symbols to enable me to enter into the mystic union. But the thing that matters in every case is the mystic union of our souls with God, in the life of Jesus. Look through everything in the service into the eyes of God.

3. DIGNIFIED WORSHIP

Next to these, and dependent on these, I place that which is frequently too much valued for itself, as if it were an independent thing—*reverence or dignity*. Reverence is entirely secondary both to joy and spirituality. The only style of reverence that can be tolerated is that which is fully consonant with Christian joy. There is a mock form of reverence, a mere manner of posture rather than a state of soul, that may smother both joy and spirituality. Dignity is a poor thing when it is only a decorum of manner or words, assumed as being appropriate and fitting.

Reverence under any definition is simply our method of approach to God. Some people approach like crawling worms, and others like a mute at a funeral. But choice souls who know the love of God in Jesus approach with a holy boldness. The one thing to be sure of in any Christian service is that there is no such thing as a reverent manner in itself. Posture, as such, has nothing to do with reverence. As Joel puts it, 'Rend your heart and not your garments.' Reverence is *an attitude of the soul*, adoring and praising God, and not an attitude of the body. It may indeed suggest fashions and methods that strive to express it or aid it. But that is an individual matter. An Easterner expresses reverence by crawling on the ground—we don't! Cultivate the reverent mind: that will suggest its own fitting expression. Buf if reverent ways help you, use them.

4. PROGRESSIVE WORSHIP

In the order of your services, *study arrangement and progress.* It is the more incumbent on us to cultivate order because we have none imposed upon us. If we would save ourselves and our people from anything haphazard, ragged or ill-balanced, we must study seemliness and progress. By order, I do not mean fixity. But each type of service should have its own typical progression and arrangement. Study as many service-books as possible: if they do not give you a definite order which you may make your own, they will at least show you the range of possibilities, and may suggest varieties of movement and progress.

But the point in any service, whatever its order or arrangement of parts, is that it should reach a climax. In the Christian view, that climax is surely this—that God in His pardoning, strengthening and directing power should be plainly visible, so that your worshippers may depart eased of their burdens and encouraged in their faith.

I often hear ministers discussing the question of 'unity' in a service. But there are two ideas of unity, one a bare and narrow unity, made so by exclusion, the other a comprehensive unity, made so by inclusion. Which of these should we aim at? Let me illustrate. I remember being present at a service where the minister preached on Christian joy. No subject, as I have assured you, could be more fitting. But the preacher had planned—narrowly, I think—to make his service a 'unity'. For this purpose he chose his hymns only from those of an exultant strain. His readings were selected from the big glad passages of Scripture. His prayers were like 'Songs in Spring', full of gratitude to God for the joy and goodness of life. The service, I admit, was a unity of a kind—but a narrow unity. In spite of the intrinsic beauty and art of the service, I could not help feeling a great sense of gaunt omission. There was not a single little niche in it all for a man with a broken or burdened heart, or for any of Christ's little ones who had bruised their feet on the cobble stones. Should that be—in any common service?

There is a bigger and better idea of unity than that. May I speak personally? If I feel that my own message is concerned chiefly with a special topic or a limited aspect of Christian life, one that may only affect a particular circle of an average audience, I try deliberately to supplement in the rest of the service what may be lacking in the sermon. Preserving a true unity, we may make the general service atone for our omissions in preaching. For instance, we may choose general broad praise. We may even select our Scripture passages from another angle, representing supplementary truth. The opening prayers of the service may even gather round the opposite sweep of our thoughts. If you desire it, the concluding praise and the last brief prayer may focus round the message of your sermon and complete the impression. By this method I feel that we do not leave any of God's big-eyed children untended and unfed, and that no wanderer need go home feeling forlorn or forgotten. This seems to me as much of a unity as the other type of service, which I admit may be suitable for special occasions. But I prefer the larger unity, defined not by what it omits but by what it includes. Contrary to common talk, I have found that people are shocked not by a man's awkward way of saying things but by his awkward way of forgetting things!

5. FREE WORSHIP

The last quality of which I have time to speak is one that is our mingled glory and peril—*freedom*. In this privilege, if wisely used, we have an undoubted gain over every type of fixed service, however beautiful it may seem. Our freedom is precious, for it is not only a freedom from forms, but a freedom, if we care, to use forms. We have the whole liturgies, rites, symbols and methods of the world at our choice. Other churches are bound. We are free—free even to bind ourselves!

This gives us a wonderful range of *adaptability*, which we may use with deft power for the changing needs and problems of the day, personal, civic and national. A 'tied church' with prescribed service and prayers may be ludicrously inappropriate or remote in any special crisis. If we use it reverently, our freedom is a gift beyond price. But it must be used with dignity and fitness, with strict impartiality and without the shadow of a bias. However, among trained men such as you are, if your hearts are prepared, there is less danger than opportunity in this fine privilege. Be quite ready, as our forefathers put it, to 'improve the occasion', so long as you avoid the temptation, in the heat of national stress, to magnify molehills into mountains.

SINGING AND READING

In closing this lecture, let me refer shortly to two items of the service. I allude to them specially, because in answer to my 'round robin' I received some pointed criticism from thoughtful laymen.

1. CONGREGATIONAL PRAISE

Many of our congregational hymns are not good, either as music, poetry or theology. 'Not good' is a mild term. They are often bad. From the organist's point of view, many of them are either a jingle or a jazz. (My organist, Dr. Hollins, sometimes says to me, 'Please don't give us that sugary tune!') From the minister's point of view, they are often crude or diseased theology, quite unworthy of the modern age. And from the people's point of view, they frequently express a strained or feverish piety that makes impossible demands on healthy-minded Christians. My sense of humour is often dangerously tickled when I see a big robust rugby-player moaning out his plaintive desire to be in Heaven! I know quite well that he has no desire to go there—yet! He wants—God honour him for it—to live a full manly Christian life, facing his daily work and enjoying God's mellow sunshine as long as Providence wills it. I think you will agree with me that the average healthy Christian has no desire to chant about 'the happy land', with harps and golden streets, or to moan about this life being a 'desert drear'.

A good Christian knows that it is God's plan for him to play a man's robust part in life, facing big calls, and living on heroic levels. Personally, it makes me squirm to sing some of our slushy sentimental rants.

Now I want to emphasise that *the selection of praise is in your hands*, and ultimately you are responsible for the conduct of the service. If you have a spiritually minded organist, I should advise you to trust him. I have been so favoured in this matter all through my ministry that I now leave as much of the praise to his guidance and suggestion as I possibly can. By trusting him, you help to train his spiritual appreciation, and he becomes a real colleague in your ministry. If you have not a good organist, trust yourself!

My friend, the Rev. Gavin J. Tait, M.A., of Paisley, who has kindly corrected these lectures in their typed form, disagrees with me heartily regarding the advice given above! To balance things and to give a rounded view, I take the liberty of inserting the note he sent me. He gives his advice to the young minister in these words:

'(1) Whether you consult your organist or not, remember that yours is the responsibility for the selection of praise.

'(2) Don't grudge any time or trouble in making your selection. It is a positive affront to God and your people to leave the selection to the few hurried minutes you have in the vestry before going into the pulpit. No part of our work is so often scamped: and no part so deserves or will so repay the most careful preparation.

'(3) In making your selection remember all the time that it is the service of *Praise* for which you are preparing. The element of Praise, Adoration, and Thanksgiving should therefore be prominent in every service. Choose the great psalms and hymns which express the glory of God in Creation, Providence and Redemption, and those which sing with triumphant note of the Incarnation, the Cross, the Resurrection, and the Glory of the Lord. These are the themes on which the Christian heart loves to utter itself in adoring praise. Introspective hymns dealing with the various phases of Christian experience have their place, of course, but it is a distinctly secondary place.

'(4) Don't neglect our metrical Psalms and Paraphrases. They have been too much neglected in recent years, since the introduction of Hymns. There are welcome signs that they are coming into their own again. They have still a great place in the affections of the Scottish people. If well chosen, and sung to our good old Scottish tunes, they will evoke a response from the people that is given to few hymns. If you have five items of praise in your service, as is commonly the case, is it too much that two of these at least should be selected from the Psalms and Paraphrases?'

I agree so much with this that I gladly insert it. Still, it doesn't really impair the advice that you and your organist should work together as colleagues. Few ministers have any knowledge of music: and your organist presumably has. It is very much better that both of you should compound your gifts, and that you should pull together sweetly, as a pair of horses yoked together in common work. If you make the selection of praise on your own behalf, however, my friend's advice is all that is to be desired.

A congregation's taste in good praise can be marvellously trained, so that it instinctively rejects what is cheap and tawdry. But its taste can be as easily debased, until the people come to regard good music as cold and austere, and delight in jingle and cheap effects. The cure is in your hands. Avoid clattering and ranty tunes: and avoid hymns that are unnatural in their aspirations, falsely pietistic or mawkishly sentimental. There are some hymns in every Church Book that should only be sung by a man in the privacy of his closet, for they are personal, not congregational hymns. Avoid too, except for unique occasions, the 'minor' in thought and music. Choose the robust, strong and manly praise which the best Christian authors have given us, with dignity of thought, broad movement and worthy aspiration—brave, heroic hymns that uplift and exalt.

In this matter—merely to show you that it is no small thing—take a lesson from history. We know that the historical beginning of the Reformation lay in the ancient hymns of the people, which in spite of Church corruptions furnished them with a saving theology. Martin Luther had enough foresight to use hymns and psalms for the edifying of his people. The two Wesleys, also, established their great Church not only on preaching but on hymns. The Roman Catholic Church in Britain, learning from us and from their own former omissions, are now teaching their young people English hymns suitable for their own faith. Thousands of children who pass through our Sunday schools have their only theology crystallised in the praise they learn in school and church. Would it not be a pity if their hymns should be sloppy in sentiment, unworthy in theology and cheap in musical appeal? This lies with you as leaders of the service. By your choice of noble, dignified and worthy praise—and we have many hymns that are matchless—you may so educate a congregation's taste that its appreciation becomes swift and fine. The appetite grows by what it feeds on.

In speaking especially to you Americans, allow me the privilege of a growl! Since I came to America on this visit, I have not once heard any of the old grand Scottish metrical psalms and paraphrases—and that too in the Presbyterian Church! Now, your fathers and our fathers—great men—were fed and reared on the psalms. There is a grandeur, both of thought and music, in many of the old Scottish psalms that makes them peculiarly suitable for congregational singing. We miss something stately in our Scottish services, if the psalms are not used. They are particularly suitable for opening or invocational praise. We are learning nowadays that the psalms are typically temple-praise; and the very absence of an individual or introspective note is a gain for united worship. They are timeless and therefore timely. I hope you will not be tempted to impoverish your services by the disuse of these ancient songs. They sustained the faith of past days in the grand note. Amid all the devious, grovelling introspectiveness of modern psychological tendencies, I feel that it is this grand note we need to recapture.

2. PUBLIC READING

A last word—not the least important—about the public reading of Scripture. I told you in an earlier lecture that before beginning my work for this course, I invited the opinion and criticism of some intelligent laymen regarding the subject of these lectures. In almost every reply, some critical mention was made of the public reading of Scripture. Some complained about *manner*, and some about *selection*. One correspondent remarked that certain preachers conveyed the impression that they had only hurriedly chosen their passages in the vestry, at random, a few minutes before entering the pulpit. Generally, it was averred that the reading of Scripture was often casual, unstudied and sometimes unintelligent.

This is a scandal. It reflects on us; it reflects on our congregation; and it reflects on our view of Scripture. It argues an unhealthy idea of our duty and function. I suppose our apparent casualness arises from the false presumption that we already know our passages well. And in any case—so we think—Scripture-reading is an easy thing. The truth is, it is the most difficult thing in the service—to do well!

I hold that the reading of Scripture cannot be regarded too seriously, especially if we think of it as the message of God and the source of our spiritual life. And for this purpose, it cannot be too studiously prepared. To have the Word nobly read is an equal joy and education for our people. After all, it is more important to hear the Word than our words about it.

May I venture to give you three general counsels out of any experience I have?

(*a*) Choose and study your passages carefully. No man can expect to read well and convey the full meaning of a chapter to others, if the meaning is not perfectly clear to himself. The secret of good reading is to get into the atmosphere of your subject, so that you not only know it but *feel* it. If you can do this, you will be easily guided in different methods of treatment for different types of subjects. For instance, narrative should be read as narrative—simple, straightforward reading, with natural stress and emphasis, sufficient to outline the story in its developments and crisis. On the other hand, a dramatic situation should be read with its own native feeling—dramatically, but reverently so. Poetry also: well, poetry is not less poetry because it is Biblical. There need be, and should be, no declamation and no laboured elocution such as one often hears in public recitations. The ideal is good, natural speech, well articulated, and delivered with reverence as the message of God to man.

Personally, for congregational purposes, I recommend the Authorised Version. Apart from other considerations, it is great literature. Moreover, its haunting words are enshrined in the world's memory.

(*b*) Read naturally, with ordinary flexibility, modulation and ease. Good reading is equal to a running commentary, and better than most. I am afraid I have not much use for the man who stops and makes a passing commentary. It needs an exceptional man to do it well. Ordinary stress in reading will do as much: it 'explains' better than our explanation.

Avoid anything stagy or rhetorical in Bible reading. I have twice asked an elocution master to read the lessons for me. Although it was fine reading, I found on each occasion that the little added touch of over-loaded emphasis annoyed the average hearer.

(*c*) Do not walk only on well-beaten tracks. There are more passages in the Bible than Isaiah 53, Luke 15, John 15, and 1 Corinthians 13! You have a duty to open up the Bible to your people. With a full selection and careful preparation, you will make the Scripture lessons a delight to your church.

I enjoyed all the *Responsive Readings* I have heard in America. But I question if the greater part of the Bible is suitable for this. The psalms, I believe, are eminently suitable: indeed, many of them were written purposely for responsive chanting. Such a practice, moreover, gives the congregation a definite part in the service.

I do not know whether anything I have said is in the least helpful for you in the conduct of your service. I have purposely avoided detailed advice and have confined myself to saving principles. Whatever form our service may take, in our own church or denomination, the main thing for all of us is that we should have a true view of the theory, purposes and opportunities of worship. With these in our minds, we shall bring to the service the one thing it needs—a prepared heart and a reverent soul.

8 Common Prayer

Resort to sermons, but to prayers most.
Praying's the end of preaching.
GEORGE HERBERT, *Church Porch*

According to Jeremy Taylor, prayer is 'an ascent of the mind to God'. If we do not import into this phrase any of our modern psychological distinctions between mind and soul and spirit, the definition may be as good as any, within the compass of a single sentence. Other writers, expressing the same thought in different terms, define prayer as 'the soul's transactions with God', 'our spiritual commerce with the infinite', 'intimacy', 'fellowship', 'communion', and in the old Biblical sense of the term, 'conversation,' our walk with God.

Humanly speaking, the origin of all prayer, reasoned or inarticulate, lies in our haunting sense of incompleteness, the mysteries that surround us from birth to death, the tragic contrast between our dreams and our powers, and the urgency of human need. Even among the least civilised people, this need is not only physical but also spiritual, involving the satisfactions of the soul as well as of the body: for the two are as bafflingly interwoven as a tangled skein. Indeed, I question if there is anything physical in us which has not its spiritual reflex.

In its most primitive form, prayer is a fierce and perhaps unreasoned cry for help, direction and peace. In all ages and even in all states of culture, men have dimly recognised that there are powers around us that are bigger than ourselves, in whose ways of working, as they clash with our desires, we find a source of constant mystery. And at times, in the hands of these powers, we and the whole human race seem as pawns on the board. When we rise up through this to some definite view of God, personal and caring, prayer becomes in its highest form a spiritual communion of man's soul with God's. And as in all other things, it is the highest form that alone explains the lowest. The lowest is always greater than it seems, just because it has the possibility of the highest locked in its heart.

Thus in its diverse modes and degrees, prayer is as wide as human life itself, and reaches back beyond all history. I have no doubt that the expression of prayer is really *the earliest form of every religion.* In their gusts of unexplainable agony, men uttered prayers before they knew why they should utter them, and certainly before they had any reasoned or even worthy idea of God. Prayer is the cry forced from a puzzled or tortured soul, as instinctive on its own plane as the yelp of a dog. Thus as a practice —although in our sophistication we may think it absent from 'primitive' religions—prayer is more primitive than the most primitive creed, for the creed only seeks to explain or formulate what the prayer instinctively assumes. I am quite sure in my own mind that it is so instinctive in its nature that it did not spring from any reasoned view of God or any sure belief in its own efficacy. The true process is rather the reverse—that men, reasoning from its instinctive practice, rose through it, and perhaps by it, to their developed views of God. In their blundering prayers, as they made their appeal to the powers that shape us, *they found God*, as one groping in the dark at last touches something solid and sure.

In this lecture there is no call to justify prayer either as reasonable or effective. To do so would involve theological issues that are clearly beyond our scope. But generally we may say that we believe in prayer because the two parties concerned are equally spirit, and spirit life is the one thing conceivable that is independent of our limiting ideas of time and space. To criticise prayer on these material issues reveals a crude mind and gross views, and most of all, betrays a fundamental misconception of *spiritual relations and values.* Indeed, all the fascinating discoveries of modern research are only lending a sweet reasonableness to prayer, as an experience not in any sense determined by the material tests of space or time. The recent discovery that the whisper of a man goes endlessly on through space, and the revelation of psychological and spiritual actions and reactions, make the call of the man-soul to the God-soul a reasonable thing. It is certainly less difficult and less incredible nowadays to think that God is listening in, and that every cry of the soul has its own 'wavelength'. The greatest gain for religion in modern research is this gain of the open mind.

WHAT IS COMMON PRAYER?

Among Christians, congregational or common prayer is the offered prayer of the gathered people. In the early days of the Church, this offering no doubt was purely spontaneous—open also to all who felt inspired. We cannot over-emphasise this *inspired freedom* in the Church of the Apostles. This being so, there was of course no appointed person to conduct or guide the worship. But as the Church grew, this lack of discipline became increasingly dangerous as a source of disorder. And so to prevent abuses and for the ends of decency, recognised people were chosen as leaders or shepherds, whose duty it was to control this public worship as presidents.

The ground and justification of common prayer may be found in that passage of St. Matthew's Gospel (18 : 19–20) where our Lord emphasises the power of *union* in prayer. 'If two of you shall agree on earth as touching anything that they shall ask, it shall be done for them of My Father which is in heaven.' Then Jesus adds our great charter for united public worship, 'For where two or three are gathered together in My name, there am I in the midst of them.' This is a promise of particular grace to be obtained, and only obtained, in public worship.

In our day and circumstances, however he may be styled, a leader of worship is clearly necessary. The duty of this leader, apart from any differing views of his place and function, is to gather up and interpret the desires and needs of his brethren, and intercede on their behalf. Even if he does not call himself a priest, he has some priestly function, for he offers the 'sacrifice of prayer' to God on behalf of others.

I admit that there is another quite valid view of what congregational prayer might be. This is found most beautifully and powerfully embodied in the Quaker idea of common prayer. Here, as I understand, the topics or range of prayer may be stated or sketched to the people, whereupon the congregation bows in silent worship. Each individual, in his own words and peculiar personal passion, entreats silently along the suggested lines in a great common harmony. This, in an ideal sense, is *common prayer*. Indeed, it is the only real common prayer. It is not one man voicing the prayers of others, but all voicing their own. It gathers up the united passion and fervency of the whole people: and it gives, what most services lack, a true place for the congregation in worship.

I might suggest that this ideal of common prayer could be helpfully welded to our own. In all types of service, liturgical or non-liturgical, is there any reason why such a fashion of worship should not be wisely introduced? If the topics of prayer are suggested by the leader, and helpfully forecast, I do not see why this method should not have an honoured place in our worship. Apart from everything else—say, its power and spirituality—it trains the congregation in personal intercession, which is the secret of any church's vitality.

OUR DIFFICULTIES

Under our type of service, the leader of common prayer, free or liturgical, is faced with peculiar difficulties. He is, and must always be, conscious of two audiences: and from this fact spring his difficulties.

On the one hand, he is aware of his human audience, the group of men and women, varied and diverse, for whom and in whose hearing he prays. The difficulty here is twofold: Firstly, to know and interpret the heart of his people aright, gathering up their needs and sorrows and joys, so that no one feels he is overlooked or forgotten. Secondly, while conscious of this audience and their needs, he must be unconscious of it in the best sense and untrammelled by it, so that while remembering his people he only remembers God. Thus he has both to remember his people and forget them, and to do both at the same time. If I may say it, the secret of most faults in common prayer lies here. Either the ministrant does not sufficiently remember the audience, or does not sufficiently forget them. He may not remember them enough, and so may make his prayers unbalanced, circumscribed or inadequate. Or he may not forget them enough, for they may hold him and bind him, influence his moods and make him self-conscious, leading him often to speak *to* them and not *for* them. It is so easy for a minister to think of impressions rather than results, of what the people are judging rather than of the ends of worship. Perhaps no mortal man, except in rare moments of ecstasy, ever quite rids himself of this sense of a human audience, or of a task discharged in their hearing.

On the other hand, he has the second audience, God. He is speaking to the divine soul of the Father. But even in addressing this high audience, he dare not forget his other audience. For he has not only to express his own personal feelings, but he must express and interpret the great common sinning and yearning heart of the world. In addressing God, he sins if he remembers the human audience too much: and he sins equally if he forgets it too much. Well may one say, 'Such things are too high for me.'

FREE OR PRESCRIBED PRAYER?

There are two diverse and contrasted ways in which the common prayers of the people may be offered: on the one hand, by means of a prepared and authorised liturgy, where the petitions and intercessions are openly read; and on the other hand, by means of free prayer where the leader—also, I hope, prepared—offers up in natural speech the needs and aspirations of the people, out of the fullness of his own heart.

As one may gather from their extended use, both methods have much to say for themselves. It is only fair for you as students to consider this question, for even although you are ministers of a church that is 'free', your freedom consists, as I cannot sufficiently urge, in a superb liberty to choose different methods as they may approve themselves to you and your people. I shall try to state the question as fairly, and as shortly, as I can: and I leave you to judge according to your wisdom and the spirit of God.

I. FOR AND AGAINST LITURGICAL PRAYER

I ask you to consider, first, what has to be said for and against a prescribed liturgy.

On the side of a liturgy, there are many precious and distinct gains.

(*a*) To begin with, any worthy prayer-service is a compendium of the great and honourable prayers of all the ages of believers. It is not one man praying, but the Church praying, the communion of saints and great souls in the long history of the Christian faith.

(*b*) A liturgy is generally exceedingly comprehensive without being diffuse, a balanced, considered and devout expression of our great common needs. It is wonderfully complete and ordered: and few souls ever feel that their desires and needs are overlooked or misrepresented.

(*c*) It is less particular and individualistic than free prayer, and is seldom personal. In other words, it is broadly human, and never errs by being curiously analytical or introspective.

(*d*) It is framed in beautiful, memorable and haunting words: and the fact that it is so often repeated and is common property gives it a hold on the congregation's memory. The people literally *pray with* the leader in words and phrases that are familiar and loved.

(*e*) It is dignified and noble in construction, never vulgar or common, never lame or halting, never abrupt or broken, never annoying to any sensitive soul.

(*f*) The congregation is saved from the excesses or disabilities of the individual leader, free from his moods and peculiarities, his eccentricities of thought and speech, his limitation of outlook, or his mental and spiritual shortcomings.

(*g*) And there is this to be said, that if the leader is reverent and *feels* the prayers he reads, they are likely to be living both to him and the worshippers. It may be more difficult to capture, but there is no reason why he should *lose*, a saving personal passion.

(*h*) Some people also find it a spiritual uplift to remember that they are worshipping in the same form and service as thousands of their fellow-Christians the wide world over.

On the other hand, there are considerations, important for spiritual life, that may be urged against prescribed prayer.

(*a*) At the outset, save on exceptional occasions and with exceptional men, it is difficult to ensure that a liturgy is not formal or frigid. It is so dignified that it is often cold, and so graven in its forms that it is often severe.

(*b*) It is totally inadequate to express the intimate and fluctuating aspirations of the average man. The fact that it is not open to change or modification makes it stereotyped.

(*c*) It perpetuates ancient forms and phrases—and sometimes, ancient theologies—that have passed out of common use, which makes it archaic and remote, especially to the younger generation.

The phrase 'Prevent us, O Lord' illustrates this: for the use of the word 'prevent' in the sense of 'going before' has entirely passed from common speech. Anatole France laments the loss of the dignified French of the previous century, but then he wisely remarks, 'Nevertheless, it is always best to speak the speech of our fellows.'

(*d*) We have talked so much about the beauty and adequacy of prayer-books that we have hypnotised ourselves into the belief that they are finer than they really are. Dr. Percy Dearmer remarks in his recent book, *The Church at Prayer*, 'Indeed, all the service books of Christendom demand considerable improvement: they spring from a period of great intellectual poverty, and though they are far better than anything else in the scanty literature between Constantine and Otto the Great, they set us wondering why the concentration of the long Medieval period upon Church matters produced so little literature of the highest quality.' And regarding the Book of Common Prayer, he adds, 'It would be strange indeed if no improvements could be made in the thought which was natural to Englishmen between the reigns of Henry VIII and James I.'

(*e*) While familiarity may endear a liturgy to many, the same familiarity, with unending repetition, may make it a mere recitation or even a 'tinkling cymbal' to others. The absence of variety or plasticity amid our changing needs is strongly felt by many minds.

(*f*) Its great lack is warmth, particular application, and personal appeal. Things can be so general and broad that they fail to touch individual hearts.

(*g*) It can well become too mechanical, cold and passionless: and consequently as a function, it may be, and often is, discharged like a lesson.

(*h*) The very fact that it is so independent of the mood or preparation of the speaker may make it dull and toneless—a prayer without a praying soul behind it, an intercession without an intercessor.

(*i*) Many urge that prescribed forms are quite unnatural for any fervid devotion, and are against the teaching and habit of our Lord and the customs of the Apostolic Church. The beauty of a Prayer Book only appeals to a class, and especially to those who have lost the first rapture of exalted love. If we are hungry children of God, this is not the way in which even reverent children address their Father.

On the whole, I believe that a liturgy is more welcomed by the speaker than by the people. Without any doubt, its historical origin lies among the clergy. A form of prayer is an untold relief to the ministrant, for it saves him from a burden of worrying responsibilities, and most of all, it saves him from himself. From long custom, it may now be sincerely welcomed by many worshippers, but originally it was a *pastor's device.* It is not a device by the people to save themselves from a poor minister: but it is a device of the clergy to save poor ministers from themselves. I sincerely doubt whether we can find the origin of the Liturgy, *as an instrument for Church devotion*, in the need to provide ignorant people with prayers for their own private use. I admit that the need must have been early felt to furnish untaught people with prayers for their own devotional life. But that is quite another affair from the use by the ministrant of prescribed prayer for *his* purposes in public worship!

2. FOR AND AGAINST FREE PRAYER

What may be said for and against free prayer?

(*a*) For what it is worth, it is claimed at the outset that free prayer is an Apostolic practice. It was not only our Lord's custom —which might not be a sufficient justification for us—but it was also the invariable habit of the disciples and converts of the early Church. Indeed, prayer was so free in the young Church, not only in method of utterance, but also in the numbers who claimed the privilege of offering it in each service, that some rules of order were quickly devised. But even where a leader was appointed, *prayer with him was still free.* The growth of liturgies of any kind was certainly a late development of the Church. *A Catholic Dictionary*, edited by Addis and Arnold, sums up the question thus: 'It may, we think, be safely inferred that there was no entire written liturgy during the first three centuries of the Church.' Those therefore who uphold free prayer claim that it is the ancient and original practice.

(*b*) It is pointed out that Jesus warned His disciples on many occasions against vain repetitions and empty forms, and defined worship as being always in spirit and in truth. And though He gave His followers the Lord's Prayer, He gave it not as a *form* but as a guide and example. (We have the Lord's Prayer not in one form but in two!)

(*c*) Free prayer is the natural speech of one soul to another, the expression of fervent need, a cry: and the most important thing in real prayer is not its form or words, and certainly not its dignity. God as Father does not expect set speeches and prescribed ways from His children, but a loving and simple approach. The finest prayers in the New Testament are the cries and tears of trusting souls.

(*d*) Free prayer has a spontaneity, a beautiful trust and a simple dignity native to itself; and above all in such earnest prayer, the element of *power*, sheer moving power, may be signally present—that spiritual passion and importunity which Christ so often commended.

(*e*) If reverently used, a prepared soul may employ free prayer so that it is capable of great heights, and in its secondary influence on the worshipping audience, may make it electrical in its effects.

(*f*) It is open, more than its counterpart, to finer tenderness, consoling power and uplifting influence: and in its very ruggedness and ardour it may not be inartistic. Where prepared and spoken out of a devotional soul, it is a thing of power. As a general rule, simple souls to whom the simplicity of Jesus is dear, find in it their one means of approach to God.

(*g*) It possesses a fine range of special adjustment to any of the sudden needs of the nation, the Church or the individual, compared with which prescribed prayer is like a tethered animal.

(*h*) Free prayer alone leaves sufficient room for the working of the Holy Spirit in drenching power.

On the other hand, free prayer may show as patently the defects of its qualities.

(*a*) It may lack any saving dignity either of language or thought—and perhaps, worst of all, of decent reserve.

(*b*) It may be, and too often is, dangerously free, bordering on irreverence, and wounding human susceptibilities and a natural feeling of decorum.

(*c*) It may err equally in what it expresses and what it omits, dealing on the one hand in curious personal points of view, and omitting on the other hand the great common desires of the human heart.

(*d*) In method its greatest peril is to be formless, ragged, slovenly and unbalanced. Personal emphasis, to which we are specially liable, may ruin all just proportion amid the needs of a mixed congregation.

(*e*) It depends too much on the personal leader, on his moods, his failings, his culture, and his individual fidelity to himself, his preparation and his God. Curiously enough, the finer and more spiritual the leader is, the more may his prayers lack any contact with ordinary needy souls, for he may soar through the heavens and leave them neglected on the earth. A congregation may need to be saved as much from the beautiful extravagances of a saintly mystic as from the dullness of an uninspired soul.

(*f*) Not only may free prayer 'meander', but it may be inordinately long. George Whitefield once said of a preacher, 'He prayed me into a good frame of mind, and then prayed me out of it!' (It is also fair to say that many prayer-books are inordinately long.)

(*g*) In the hands of one who is either unprepared or inexpert, it may touch depths only equalled by its heights. I have heard prayers that made me shiver, which were only saved from irreverence by their evident sincerity and passion.

I have tried to express as fairly as I can the powers and possibilities of the two methods, upward and downward. If I might speak personally, I have been greatly stirred and impressed by some liturgies: but I have never been moved just so much as by free prayer in the hands of a fine reverent soul touched by the spirit of God, as the wind ruffles water. One may easily assert that a liturgy is *safe*, for it will never sink so low as free prayer. But on the other hand, it may never rise so high. Generally, there are situations where only one or the other seems suitable. In a stately service, in some ancient abbey or cathedral, I should prefer the one. That is the natural home of the liturgy, where it intones through the aisles as the wind moans through the trees. But in the usual services of the ordinary congregation, I should never desire anything finer than reverent, untrammelled prayer, finely done.

Whether a combination of the two for an ordinary service is either possible or desirable, I leave to your own wisdom. Our gain, as ministers of a church 'free', is our ability to form and order our own service. If we cared to exercise the privilege of making a judicious selection of the best prayers and forms of the general Church, *with the principle of free prayer fully preserved*, we might evolve a type of worship that might easily surpass any of the prescribed and fixed services of any or all of the churches. Meanwhile, many of our ministers who practise free prayer have an unconscious liturgy of their own, lines of thought and expression as fixed as any printed routine, with the grave disadvantage, however, of having neither beauty, dignity nor adequacy.

THE PRINCIPLES OF FREE PRAYER

With this said, we may leave the question of a liturgy alone, for it needs no special preparation for its use except the extreme preparation of a man's own heart. If any of us do employ prescribed forms in our own particular worship, let us be only the more certain that we bring to their use an exalted soul, that we may read into the cold words of print our own redeeming passion.

But preparation—distinct, methodical and constant—is needed for free prayer. The common tragedy, and the source of most of its glaring faults, is to consider free prayer *unprepared prayer*. In all conscience why should a man prepare so sedulously to address his fellow men, and come so casually to his God? We need preparation, first and last—the prepared soul, the prepared mind, and even the prepared word—when we come into the House of God to offer the sacrifices of the people to their Lord. Nothing less than this is worthy of Him, of us, of our work and of our people.

In line with the plan I adopted when speaking to you about sermon-work, may I now, for convenience of treatment, divide this preparation into two headings, *general* and *special*.

I. GENERAL PREPARATION

(*a*) The first regulative thing in our preparation of prayer, giving us one great condition of power, is *a simple assurance of its need and efficacy*. Unless prayer is real to us—not a mere piece of work to be performed, but a unique opportunity and privilege—it cannot possibly have any appeal to others. Moreover, this belief alone gives us a true incentive towards adequate preparation, and imparts that commanding note of reality in its exercise that is unmistakable. It saves us from the 'office' of the ministry, and gives us its passion.

(*b*) But further, we need a true idea not only of the efficacy of prayer, but also of its *nature and purpose*, and the qualities it demands in us. In its essence, prayer, all prayer, private or common, is an address to God where we seek to align ourselves with His will, and enter into living communion with Him. It is ruinous to think that we offer prayer to twist or argue an unwilling or an unheeding God round to our will: or to persuade Him to act grudgingly: or to cajole Him to do things He otherwise would not do: or even to remind Him of His promises, or recall His wandering attention to our needs. But if prayer is anything, it is our attempt to comprehend His will and bring our own into gracious harmony, so that we are made fit to receive the blessing He is only too ready to bestow. I do not say that prayer has only or mainly a subjective effect on us, putting us into tune with God and making us fit to receive His grace; but I do say that one great condition of gain is that we should know God's mind and pray ourselves into it.

I have heard in congregational prayer some petitions which, if answered, would ruin God's moral government of His world, and requests for Him to do the impossible—impossible because His very character forbids them. God is self-limited by His own nature!

Regarding these and other conditions of blessing in our common prayer, I may sum them up as follows: (1) a humble and reverent soul, (2) a knowledge of God's mind in Jesus, (3) the spirit of forgiveness for others, without which we cannot hope to receive the gift for ourselves, and (4) a faith that expects.

(*c*) Following this as effect follows cause, we need *a clear idea of our own special functions as ministers*. We may not call ourselves priests, in either the pagan or Jewish sense, but we claim a priestly function. We carry and uphold others, and bring their needs as seeking children to God. It is our privilege to be their voice, and to interpret their inarticulate heart. In a Christian sense there is a great parity of all souls before God, *a priesthood of believers:* but in a true sense, we hold a *priesthood for believers*. If we realise this, it will impart a high seriousness to us and a needed dignity and responsibility to our office. If we are good men, we shall study in all ways not to be unworthy of our trust; and above all things, we shall seek to avoid the sin of taking our duties slackly or perhaps the greatest temptation of all, regarding our duties as a routine.

This conception of our function and privilege is so regulative for our work, that I should write this sentence in letters of gold,

'*Magnify your office.*' Not the office itself, perhaps, but its opportunities and privileges. There would be fewer sins of casual preparation on our part did we realise, as we ought, our function for our expectant people. And always remember that we are *for the people.* This will banish intrusive individualism.

(*d*) In leading the prayers of the people, we need to cultivate first of all and most of all, *the habit and atmosphere of prayer* in our own hearts. This implies the care of our own devotional life, so that prayer is not something alien or strained, a frame of mind into which we must jerk ourselves for the moment, but is the natural and easy expression of our own trusting and seeking soul. Of them all, this type of inner preparation is the one that will most determine our power of helpfulness. Fortunately this is a gift that can be cultivated and strengthened like any other gift of man, most of all by practice, in this case the practice of the presence of God.

There is a rich and beautiful word often used in past days to describe the mysterious power in prayer that comes from this atmosphere. Our fathers called it 'unction'—that fervent quality in word and tone caused by deep religious emotion. Where this is real, it is always a power: where it is affected or forced, it is nauseous. The word, and the thing itself, have fallen into undeserved derision, simply because—being a thing of such power—those who did not have it replaced it by all kinds of futile imitations. But if only the deep religious emotion is in our hearts, the fervour of word and tone will be as natural as it is impressive.

Speaking of this fervency of spirit, Bishop Hall remarks, 'It is not the arithmetic of our prayers, how many they are: not the rhetoric of our prayers, how eloquent they be: not the geometry of our prayers, how long they may be: nor the music of our prayers, how sweet our voice may be: nor the logic of our prayers, how argumentative they may be: nor the method of our prayers, how orderly they may be: nor even the divinity of our prayers, how good the doctrine may be, which God cares for. He looks not for the horny knees which James is said to have had through the assiduity of prayer. We might be like Bartholomew, who is said to have had a hundred prayers for the morning and as many for the evening, and yet all might be of no avail. Fervency of spirit is that which availeth much.'

(*e*) Beyond this, any one who would adequately lead common prayer must be *immensely human.* I said in an earlier lecture that no one could preach usefully without a real knowledge of the human heart: but a thousand times more, no one can *pray* adequately who is apart from the stress of his fellows. The leader of prayer must remember the infinite variety in an average congregation, the varied homes and duties from which they come and the cares and problems that line their brow. We must interpret their dreams for them. We must know their sins and their heroisms, their joys and their secret sorrows, and the lusts that woo them. I remember a beautiful description of an old minister, given me by one of his people. 'When he closed his eyes in prayer, we felt as if his hands were out groping lovingly, and touching our heart-strings: and whatever he touched he soothed.' I like that picture of a sympathetic hand feeling tenderly for the sorrows and needs of other men. It suggests to me the cool hand of some loved one laid on a fevered brow. If we pray only out of our little experience or out of our own narrow goodness, we shall leave a large part of our people whose lives are untouched and whose ideals and despairs are unexpressed.

(*f*) For this end, we must study to acquire *some gift of expression*—chaste, dignified and yet supple. I do not refer here to what we call 'literary expression'. Personally, I think that one common failing of free prayer is that it is often too literary, both in form and manner. (I have even heard ministers dragging in snippets of poetic quotation which offend devotional souls.) But the leader of worship should cultivate ease and grace of speech so that he may frame his petitions in simple and memorable words. For this end, a knowledge of the Bible, with its dignity and breadth and classic speech, is clearly foremost. It is amazing to notice how many of our greatest writers, on their own profession, owe their simple dignity and flexibility of language to an intimate knowledge of the Scriptures. I do not recommend a parrot use of Bible language and phrases, whereby our prayers become merely a clever patchwork of Biblical expressions. To begin with, that becomes woefully hackneyed after a time: and further, a prayer wholly composed of Bible phrases is too remote from modern ways of speech, particularly with the young. But if we are familiar with the devotional parts of the Bible, they will give a tone, a colour, and an atmosphere that will affect us in our own devotion.

(*g*) Beyond that, even though he may never use them, I recommend each student to buy and read *every good book of devotion* on which he can lay his hands. These books represent the great souls of the Church at prayer, Christ's folk on their knees: and these men and women are saints who have sinned and sorrowed like us, and have won through to a great peace. In their prayers, which are such beautiful songs of praise, they adore our God and praise our Saviour. These may well be our example and model, both in the matter and method of prayer.

A wise man will find much direction in these books, especially regarding form. For instance, the short opening prayer of adoration, and perhaps the brief prayer (if you have it) after sermon, might be modelled mainly on the *Collect* form of the prayer-book. That form is as fixed and yet as pliable within limits, as the sonnet is in literature. Dr. Percy Dearmer wrote of it thus:

'To say that a collect has typically four parts does, none the less, help us best to understand its structure. Those parts are: (1) The Invocation of God's name, which with us generally comes first. (2) The Relative Clause, containing some reference to the divine character, or the occasion or intention of the prayer, such as "who art always more ready to hear than we are to pray." (3) The Special Petition, which may be accompanied by (3A), a Second Petition, if that second one is logically related to the first, but not otherwise: a prayer containing a collection of different petitions is not a Collect. (4) The Statement of the Purpose for which grace is asked, such as "that we may always serve Thee in pureness of living and truth." To this is added (5), the ending, a pleading of the merits of Christ, or an ascription of praise to Him which recognises His power to obtain an answer to the supplication.'

This 'sonnet-form' for the opening prayer need not be a hindrance, and may be a help, if you use your own suitable ascriptions and petitions, week by week.

(*h*) Further, regarding form, these books will teach you the *ordering of your petitions* so that your prayers may be a unity of progress, descending perhaps from the general needs of the world, the kingdom, the nation, the Church, Society, the city, the family to the individual: or, if need be, rising from the latter to the former. Order of thought, i.e. progress as against anything haphazard or unconnected, is as much a necessity of prayer as of speech. We expect our people to follow or rather accompany us in prayer: and that is only possible when natural order or movement is resident in our own thought.

(*i*) Still further, these books of prayer, besides giving us natural dignity of address, will help to save us from the crime of being too *individual* or *personal* in congregational devotion. A certain remoteness, or at least a general note rather than anything personal or particular, should be present in common worship—i.e. if it is *common worship*! Occasionally—and here our elasticity and freedom tell—an individual tone or application may be as powerful as it is helpful; but generally, in public worship the whole varied people in there common needs are to be remembered.

I advise you, therefore, to have a good acquaintance with devotional literature, remembering however that the best of it is confined within the covers of the Bible. We often speak lightly of a man having 'a gift of prayer', as if it were something that came to him by chance and for which he deserves no credit. But you will generally find that any man who has this gift has steeped himself in the Bible and in devotional literature until prayer has become both a habit and an atmosphere.

(j) Your language almost unconsciously will be subtly different from ordinary speech. The occasion itself, the weight of your function, and the remembrance of Him you address and those for whom you speak, will effect this difference for themselves, even although you may believe as a theory that your words should be simple, direct and homely. Generally, your language cannot be too simple and unaffected: but even then, the occasion itself will impart a certain dignity, sobriety and even aloofness that are not undesirable. Robert Louis Stevenson in his beautiful layman's prayers has shown us what power and appeal may lie in ordinary unofficial language. These prayers of Stevenson are of equal beauty and penetration.

Beyond these general preparations lies *the preparation of your people*. I have tried already to show you that you may train your congregation, by advice and discourse, into a devotional frame of mind and worshipful ways. An expectant people is the greatest secret of atmosphere. There are congregations that would baffle the Apostle Paul, where prayer seems like a bird with a broken wing that flutters up—and flutters down! And there are other churches where it seems as easy to pray as to breathe, where prayer indeed is as the breath of the soul. Try to strengthen this prayer-sense among your people. It may be your Bannockburn or your Flodden.

2. SPECIAL PREPARATION

I advised you in an earlier lecture to keep a book of texts and subjects for sermons. May I advise you also to keep a book for petitions and prayers? One of my own friends whose prayer-service is noted for its fullness and beauty has done this for many years. He keeps a little pocket-book in which he often jots down thoughts and phrases, fresh petitions or new schemes for prayer. If he has been visiting some case of deep distress, if he has been specially impressed with the loneliness of certain people, if the daily press is full of class strife and warfare, or if some great crisis or disaster has filled men's hearts, he there and then jots down some remembrance in prayer. (When I preached at Glasgow University, the late Professor Cooper, who conducted the devotions of the students, referred in prayer in his own beautiful way to two murderers then under sentence of death in Glasgow gaol. I do not remember ever experiencing such a sympathetic concord in prayer as at that moment.) This preparation through the week and this timeliness of prayer may mean much for the exaltation of the service and for our own spiritual efficiency. Certainly the prayers that are richest and most helpful on Sunday are the fruit of the week's labour and devotion. God uses and owns all thoughtful preparation.

Have we any right to leave our prayers to what we call *inspiration*, which in Dr. Denney's phrase is so often *desperation*? It savours of a kind of spiritual impertinence for a man to come up to church with a sermon in his head and no prayers in his heart; or for lack of definite preparation, to drop into well-worn paths and trudge lumberingly along. Many of our people, fresh from the battle and often sick with defeat, come to service with a wistful hope that through us God may whisper something to their souls. I think their greatest desire—how human it is!—is to feel that they are understood and remembered. Unless we have been with the Master of Souls in preparation, I hardly see how our people's expectation is to be realised.

But let me state that by prepared prayer I do not imply necessarily a prayer written out and memorised. A memorised prayer may be as lifeless as a memorised sermon, the chatter of words. But prepared prayer means one thing at least—that we as leaders should know precisely *what we wish to pray for*, and perhaps *how we wish to express our prayer*. We are coming to God to ask for certain definite gifts and blessings. Is it too much to ask that we should know what these are, and how we shall frame our requests?

(*a*) Our first need is a deliberate *choice of subjects for prayer*, whatever is either urgent or necessary, the special 'sacrifice' we wish to offer in the people's name. Although congregational prayer should be comprehensive, comprehensive enough at least to leave no glaring omissions, yet at any one service and on any one Sunday we cannot pray for everything. In the sailor's phrase, it is foolish for us to 'box the compass', hoping to attain an impossible completeness. We should have some such general petitions for blessing, guidance and pardon as will cover generously the needs of most: but after that, there must be a selection of special requests that seem fitting and urgent. If you have had the congregation's needs in your thoughts during the week—say in that note-book I mentioned—this selection and emphasis will be so natural as to be self-suggesting. The divisions that are common in congregational prayer will gather their own topics around them—Adoration and Thanksgiving, Confession and Pardon, Petition and Supplication. Under these or other forms, group your ideas and pleas for the day's services.

(*b*) The word 'group' suggests the next preparation—a *plan or progress of development*, through the whole service and through each separate prayer.

So far as my own ideas for progression through the morning service are concerned, I like to open Public Worship with a short Prayer of Adoration, ending with a petition for blessing and light. This prayer, I think, might well assume the Collect form, as sketched earlier in this lecture. Thanksgiving and praise for God's mercies suggest themselves as the subject of the following prayer, which with me generally passes into the subject of greatest thanksgiving—Jesus and the benefits made ours in Him, especially pardon through confession, deliverance, and new grace. For intercession, formerly called the Long Prayer—I hope it has ceased to exist under that name. Should any prayer be 'long'? Indeed, I incline to think that five minutes is enough for most prayers. For one thing, an important thing, the people cannot follow much longer. I should much rather have three or four *very short* prayers than one long one—well, for what used to be called the Long Prayer, I reserve the petitions and supplications that are in my heart for the Kingdom and the People. I invariably follow the sermon with a short collect for blessing and grace. This I think, is the usual, and natural, progress in most services. The Benediction represents 'Depart in peace'.

But in addition to this, there ought to be a definite progress and development *in each prayer*. All good thinking has order and growth; and prayer as thinking should also have it. With progress in our minds, we are more likely to be comprehensive and less likely to be omissive. For the people also it provides a natural scheme of advance or movement by which they may accompany the leader in his petitions and make them their own. Nothing is so irritating to an orderly mind as disarrangement or lack of cohesion.

You will observe this quality of progress finely illustrated in every good prayer-book. Study the schemes of movement revealed in these prayers, and notice how they pass from point to point, from subject to subject, and from class to class. But also I recommend you to form your own schemes. A fresh plan of prayer in your own mind acts like a kind of revelation. From your remarks to me concerning my previous lectures, I know that you value personal experience in these matters. May I therefore take the liberty of mentioning to you one of my own methods in this regard?

3. MOTIF PRAYERS

(*a*) For your consideration, I give you this method which I adopt, especially at an evening service, for a short general prayer. I choose first a mould of words—say, a single short sentence—and then I run this formula through the whole prayer, like the motif in a piece of music. For instance, I may take the phrase, 'Let there be light.' I ask myself in the quietness of my own room some such questions as these—'Whence comes light? Why do we need it? Where do we need it most?' At once, under this motif, helpful divisions will suggest themselves to your prayerful mind. We need light (1) In this big darkened world, with its problems and warring passions and the mysteries both of goodness and iniquity: (2) Among the counsels of the nations, where jealousy, hatred and revenge are so potent and so alarming: (3) For our own land, amid its political and social stresses—a petition for good men and good laws: (4) Among the diverse classes of people, who look askance at each other and so often misunderstand each other: (5) For the work and duties of the Church, that we may be true to conscience and alive to opportunities: (6) In our cities and glens, that wise ways may prevail and Christian ideals may be honoured: (7) Amid the anxieties and personal problems of a man's vexed life—his business, home and pleasure.

It is an ordinary and formal division: but gathered up under this new mould, it may become fresh. Such a prayer, under rough headings, might run like this: *Address*—to God, the giver of all light: who desires that all men should live in the light: Who has given us Jesus, the Light of the world. *Our Need*—for our dark and tortuous ways: to cleanse, as the pure enemy of all disease: to subdue passion and wilful ways: to guide, lest we stumble in our own folly: to reveal all good and precious things to our eyes, and to teach us to love them.

Then each or any of the suggested divisions may be taken, enlarged according to need or according to the urgency of the times, and each section finished with the petition, 'Lord, let there be light by Thy good grace.'

Again—I am only illustrating my own method, though it may be badly!—I may take the phrase, 'God was in Christ, reconciling the world unto Himself.' Here, in the *Address*, we praise God for His gracious love, evidenced in all things but perfectly in Jesus who came amongst us showing us God's mind. Then as before I ask myself, 'What do we see in Jesus thus revealed? What has God shown us in this world spectacle?'

One may take many divisions for this comprehensive hymn of praise. Let us choose one on broad lines, which may be amplified as the leader cares:

(1) In Jesus, Thou hast shown us *Thyself*—Thy superb purposes for the world, Thy pure will, Thy mercy, and Thy matchless grace. In Him, we hear God's heart calling to our souls, God who alone fulfils all that our souls demand.

(2) In Him Thou hast shown us *what we ourselves are*—our nature and our meagre life. We were pleased in poor ways until we looked in those eyes. Thereafter we see: Our need of forgiveness, for our lives are stained. Our need of daily guidance for we are wilful wanderers. Our own confidence betrays us: our ignorance leads us into sin: our fore-shortened views turn us to wrong goals: we have distorted values: our angers and jealousies embitter life. Our need of hope, the dream of God's love: a future for us and for those we have loved and lost: something for which we can live bigly and die gladly.

(3) In Him Thou hast shown us gloriously *what we shall yet be*: here in this life, by character fashioned by Him, and for ever in His fulfilling presence. Though weak, we are not defeated: though sinning, we are not lost. Thou, O Lord, even by Thy disciplines, wilt bring us one day to His feet, a finished thing.

Once more, I may take that thought so often repeated by Our Lord, 'I am the door.' I take this as a dominant idea and work it out for myself, so that under it I can comprehend many of the needs of my people. First of all, I remember that a door leads two ways. If I pass in by Jesus, I pass *from* something *to* something. What may this mean for me and my people?

If I were using this moulding phrase, I might treat it in some such way as this: *Address*—to God, the Father of Souls, in whom there is mingled knowledge and understanding, even of our weakness and sin: who so loves our welfare that He has given us Jesus to be our Lord and Guide, that very Jesus who knew our problems, our joys and our despairs.

(1) We come to Thee from the world's work and our task of living—tired and stained by the dust of our travel. Many who are young are alive to life's joys and yet are unsaved from its perils; others are overborne by its constant pressure: some even are poignantly aware of monotony and drudgery, unrelieved by prospects and cleansing dreams.

May Jesus our Lord be the door by which we enter into rest, finding new courage and a fresh consecration.

(2) We come to Thee from the world's pleasures. Some of us have sinned to buy them; many have found them vain and profitless; all of us, even though we know it not, are seeking finer satisfactions.

May Jesus our Lord be the door by which we enter into a containing happiness that is above all storm and stress.

(3) We come to Thee from the world's temptations. We know it is Thy will that we should thus be tested: but Lord, we are hard beset! Our hearts are torn with our own indecisions: we have played with foolish things, as children with fire: some of us have touched pitch and are defiled. About us are the chains of habits: and we are held by our own follies.

May Jesus our Lord be the door by which we enter into the peace of forgiveness and the higher peace of mastery, that mastery which comes from Thy mastery of us.

(4) We come to Thee from the world's cares and sorrows. There are many now before Thee who are broken things: some whose lives are an infinite ache: some with griefs that Thou alone canst heal.

May Jesus our Lord be the door by which we enter into composure and courage, and the hope that maketh not ashamed.

This type of prayer under a containing mould of words—each section amplified as seems fitting, and others added if necessary—can be made as broad and comprehensive as the leader cares. There is room in it for fine variety—for variety does not consist only in the topics we choose, but also in our method. It is not fresh subjects in the way of queer out-of-the-way petitions—generally very personal and introspective—that we wish to find, but rather new and helpful ways of presenting the age-long cries of the heart,

Now I have only ventured to mention my own practice to you, because you are fellow-students. My one desire is to show you how you may 'plan your work and work your plan'—and that on your own lines. I trust that in saying these things I have not shown you only the machinery. But there is nothing wrong with machinery, if it does real work! There is machinery in every constructed prayer: the only fault is when the machinery is either obvious or bad.

I said that I adopted this method chiefly at an evening service. The prayers at this service may well be less formal, comprehensive or elaborate. This is the more needed if the second service is to possess a different character from morning worship, which is usually more sedate and perhaps formal. Incidentally, I think the secret of a successful second service consists in such a plain distinction as I have suggested. The distinction may show itself in other ways than in prayers—in the music, for instance, and also in your style of preaching, which may well be more spoken than read. However, in answer to a suggestion, I hope to refer to the problem of the second service at the close of this lecture.

(*b*) With the subjects of your petitions chosen, and then suitably arranged and ordered, I should advise you at the beginning of your ministry to write your prayers out, word for word. In no place is halting speech or nervousness, which often lead to diffuseness and vain repetition, more out of place than in prayer. I should make sure, if I were you—personally I did so in my first few years—that your prayers are even more prepared than your sermon. Write them out, if only as a mere training in devotion and devotional language. A fellow-minister of mine, the richness of whose devotional mind I have often admired, told me of his early experience in his first country charge. An old farmer met him one day and remarked with that charming country frankness which helps as much as it humbles us, 'Aye, Mr. ——, ye are a bonny preacher, but man! ye canna pray.' As my friend remarked, the sting lay in the fact that the charge was true! But from that moment he applied himself carefully to the devotional side of his service, and by a faithful use of his gifts, he has now made himself a power in prayer. Write your prayers out, as faithfully as you prepare your sermons. You need not repeat them or memorise them: but a constant training in ordered prayer is a wonderful instrument. It will give you a deft use of fine, simple language. It will save you from slackness, from any taint of cheapness or vulgarity, from dangerous familiarity, from vain repetition, from ruts, and from anything that offends. And most of all—for you then have a measure in your own hands—it will rescue you from inordinate length. Unprepared prayer is generally long!

(*c*) Regarding your voice, study to have no affectation of manner, no whine and no drone. Intonation of any kind, which may be necessary for audibility in a large cathedral, is not needed or welcomed in a church of average size. Moreover, intonation, in addition to giving a suspicion of artificiality, is perilously near to monotony. Some ministers by their lugubrious drawl give one the impression that prayer is a state of misery. Use your natural voice subdued by the remembrance that you are addressing God. Nowhere is a restraining, simple reverence more in place than in the prayers you offer at God's throne.

4. QUALITIES AND FAULTS

Before I close, I should like to gather up some points under this heading.

(*a*) The qualities in prayer that must never be sacrificed are these:

The note of reality, on which depends true earnestness. You are not performing a function or discharging a duty, but you are engaged in the real business of a commerce of souls.

The note of spirituality, which will destroy formalism and save you from the tragedy of routine.

The note of expectant faith, which will remove mountains, and subjectively, will impart any needed ardour to your conduct of devotion.

(*b*) Some faults to be chary of are these:

Hackneyed, lifeless phrases, however pious, which express no genuine emotion in him who prays.

Prayers that instruct God, giving Him information or direction which is presumably needless.

Prayers that preach—or worse, prayers that *preach at* somebody.

The most ghastly of all—*eloquent prayers.* There is an infamous sentence that once appeared in an American paper describing a public service. Speaking of a certain minister's prayer, the reporter said, 'This was the most eloquent prayer ever delivered to a Boston audience.' That sentence of inspired journalese sums up within its small compass many of the scandals of prayer. In the first place, a prayer should never be *eloquent.* In the second place, it is not *delivered.* And in the third place, it is not *addressed to an audience*, even a Boston audience.

THE PROBLEM OF THE SECOND SERVICE

As I close this lecture, allow me to fulfil my promise regarding the question of the second service. This problem is becoming increasingly difficult to solve. Some people in America solve it in two ways: one, by not having it at all; and the other by turning it into a concert, more or less sacred. I think I prefer the former to the latter.

At the outset we have to recognise that we live in changed days, where there are changed emphases and changed ideas. The old compulsion of worship has gone—perhaps happily, for it leaves our services clean from pretension, hypocrisy and the hard hand of social proprieties. Also the old ideas of Sabbath observance have gone, happily too, and yet unhappily. Happily, in this sense—it means, for Scotland at least, that 'black Sunday' with its rigours and its 'drawn blinds' has passed for ever. But unhappily—for as so frequently happens, the good has perished in common ruin with the bad—in the swing of the pendulum some people have forgotten what Sunday means. For these and other reasons, we cannot expect the formal double attendance of past days.

What can we do to help the present situation?

(*a*) I suggest in the first place that the appeal of the second service should be made definitely to young men and women. Already where these evening services are succcessful, they do appeal definitely to young people, and are mostly attended by them.

(*b*) This suggests different methods and a different form of service. For one thing, the conduct of worship should be less formal. So far as the sermon itself is concerned, this may be effected by more popular subjects—the problems, temptations and ideals of young people. (But keep to the Gospel: it is big enough. And avoid any taint of sensationalism. That never pays, and it soon runs dry.) So far as method of speech is concerned, I recommend a freer style than is usual in the morning service. For myself, I try to vary my methods by 'reading' in the morning and 'speaking' at night.

(*c*) The music might be fuller and heartier. The old Hebrew word for praise, Hallel, meant a *loud noise*, i.e. general, hearty singing. A good deal of our congregational praise is whispered! I deprecate, however, the invasion of music, especially of the purely choral type. Frankly, the average young man or woman is not musical: and unfortunately, those who are musical are already well catered for by Sunday evening concerts.

(*d*) I have already suggested that there might be a difference in our style of prayer—certainly less formal, freer, with a more intimate and personal note. I cannot tell you how many people—of course they may only represent a class—have told me that they derive more uplift from an evening service of this kind than from the formal service of the morning.

CONCLUSION

Gentlemen, my work is done. I have enjoyed digging again into my own mind and experience, for I think that thereby I have helped myself. I only hope that in the process I may have helped some of you.

Regarding the whole field covered by these talks, I am sure of one thing. Our work is big enough for us to use all the preparation and all the talent we can bring to its discharge. I have tried in our discussions to show you a full horizon. This work is a great concern to my own soul, and I would not be in any other line of life if I could change to-morrow. There may be restrictions placed on us by the duties of our calling, and perhaps many annoying economies.

But if any of the passion of Jesus be in us, we shall find countless subtle compensations. And our reward is with us. If we keep near to God, our pleasure in our work will grow with the passing years, and if we submit our gifts to His grace, He will use us for big things. Meanwhile, yours will be the care and shepherding of souls. Bring to it all the enthusiasm and passion of your own rich life. That is the only secret of growing power and personal joy. I pray that you may have great happiness and reward in your work, wherever God may call you. But your work well done will be its own best reward.

I thank you sincerely for the gentle hearing you have given me throughout these lectures, and especially for your condoning patience with much that must have seemed obvious.

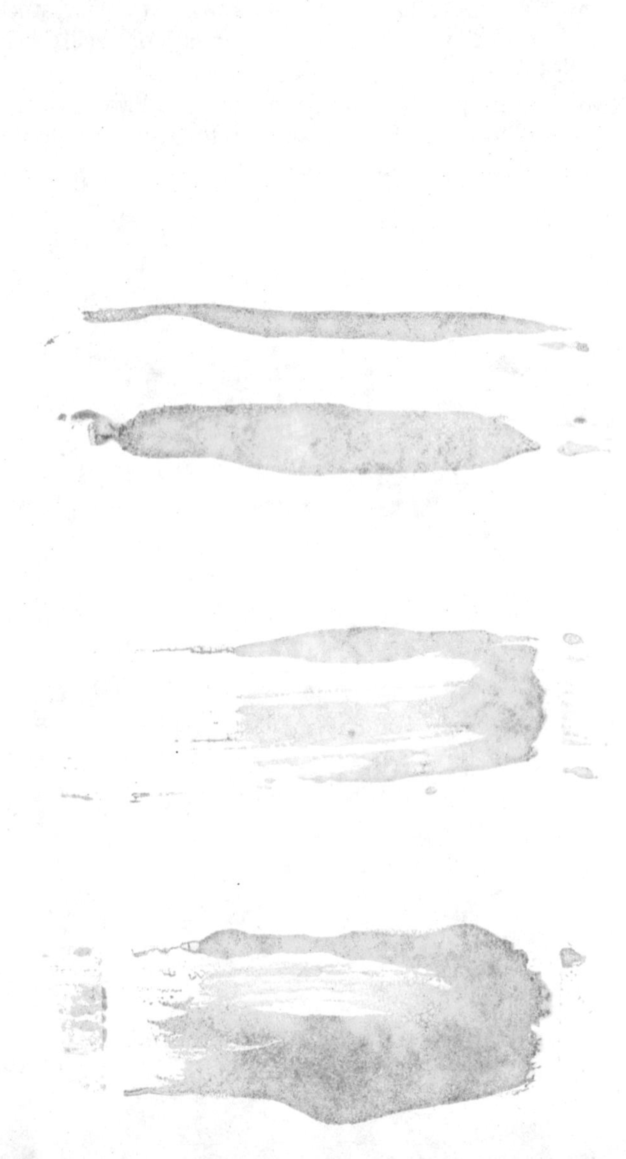